The Prosperity Mindset
Transforming Financial Myths Into Wealth Realities

By: Zenovia Cooks

"But remember the LORD your God, for it is he who gives you the ability to produce wealth, and so confirms his covenant, which he swore to your ancestors, as it is today."

Deuteronomy 8:18

Copyright

Copyright 2024 by Zenovia Cooks, Realtor DRE 02127722

All rights reserved

Dedication

To all the Participants and Clients,

"I have had the privilege of working with you in various capacities within nonprofit organizations. This book is dedicated to you. Your resilience, stories, and unwavering spirit have been my muse and inspiration throughout this journey. It is through our shared experiences that I have gained invaluable insights and a deeper understanding of the profound impact of community and support. My hope is that this book serves as a tool for education and empowerment, not only for you but also for myself, as we continue to learn and grow together. Thank you for being a part of this journey and for inspiring me to create this work."

Table of Contents

Introduction 1

Chapter 1: Debunking the Myth of Instant Prosperity 3

Chapter 2: Challenging Limiting Beliefs About Wealth 18

Chapter 3: Mindset Matters 33

Chapter 4: Understanding Wealth Creation 51

Chapter 5: Embracing Entrepreneurship as a Path to Prosperity 74

Chapter 6: The Power of Strategic Investing 91

Chapter 7: Financial Literacy and Empowerment 101

Chapter 8: Embracing True Prosperity 126

Conclusion 132

Additional Information 134

About the Writer 158

Notes 159

Introduction

In a world captivated by instant gratification and get-rich-quick schemes, the true nature of prosperity often remains elusive. For years, I've witnessed countless individuals fall prey to misconceptions about wealth creation, believing they can pray their way to riches, misunderstanding the fundamentals of wealth, or desperately seeking instant fortune through gambling. These misguided beliefs not only lead to financial disappointment but also obscure the path to genuine prosperity. Breaking Limiting Beliefs for" Abundant Success: A Journey to Financial Empowerment" emerges from a pressing need to address these widespread misconceptions and offer a clear, actionable roadmap to financial well-being.

This book aims to challenge the myths that have long clouded our understanding of wealth and replace them with empowering truths that can transform lives. Throughout these pages, we'll embark on a journey to redefine prosperity, uncover Limiting Beliefs and move beyond the narrow confines of monetary wealth to embrace a more holistic view of success and fulfillment. We'll explore the foundations of wealth creation, delve into the power of entrepreneurship, and uncover the transformative potential of strategic investing.

We'll emphasize the critical role of financial literacy in empowering individuals to take control of their financial destinies. As we debunk the myth of instant prosperity, you'll discover that true wealth is not a matter of luck or magical thinking, but a result of informed decisions, disciplined action, and a mindset geared toward long-term success. We'll examine real-world examples of individuals who have navigated the complex terrain of wealth creation, learning from both their triumphs and setbacks. This book is not just about accumulating money; it's about cultivating a prosperity mindset that permeates all aspects of life. It's about understanding that real wealth encompasses financial security, personal growth, meaningful relationships, and the ability to make a positive impact on the world around us. Whether you're just starting your financial journey or looking to reorient your approach to wealth," Breaking Limiting Beliefs for Abundant Success: A Journey to Financial Empowerment"offers practical insights, strategies, and tools to help you navigate the path to true prosperity. By the time you turn the final page, you'll be equipped with the knowledge and mindset to transform financial myths into wealth realities, paving the way for a more secure and fulfilling future. Let's begin this transformative journey together, challenging old assumptions and embracing new perspectives on what it truly means to prosper in today's world.

Chapter 1: Debunking the Myth of Instant Prosperity

The allure of instant prosperity has captivated human imagination for centuries. From ancient alchemists seeking to turn lead into gold to modern-day lottery enthusiasts dreaming of life-changing jackpots, the desire for quick and effortless wealth seems deeply ingrained in our collective psyche. However, this persistent myth of instant prosperity is not only unrealistic but potentially harmful to our financial well-being and personal growth. In this chapter, we'll explore the origins of this myth, its manifestations in contemporary society, and the reasons why embracing a more realistic approach to wealth creation is crucial for long-term success and fulfillment. The myth of instant prosperity also ignores the crucial role of financial education and literacy in building wealth. Many people lack basic understanding of budgeting, investing, and long-term financial planning, which are essential skills for creating and maintaining wealth. This knowledge gap makes individuals more susceptible to misleading promises of quick riches and less likely to engage in the disciplined practices necessary for genuine financial growth. Another overlooked aspect is the importance of developing multiple income streams and diversifying investments. Sustainable wealth often comes from a combination of sources, including earned income, passive income from investments, and potentially business ownership. This diversification not only increases financial stability but also provides opportunities for compound growth over time.

The instant prosperity myth also fails to account for the role of networking and relationship-building in financial success. Many wealthy individuals attribute a significant portion of their success to connections made over years or decades. These relationships often lead to business opportunities, mentorship, and valuable insights that can't be replicated through any get-rich-quick scheme.

The myth also disregards the psychological aspects of wealth management. Suddenly acquiring a large sum of money without the mental preparation and discipline to manage it responsibly can lead to poor decision-making and rapid loss of wealth. This phenomenon is often seen in lottery winners who find themselves worse off financially within a few years of their windfall. Let's take a look at Jack:

Jack couldn't believe his eyes when he saw the matching numbers on his lottery ticket. He had just won $10 million. Overnight, the 32-year-old factory worker became a multi-millionaire. At first, Jack was cautious. He paid off his modest mortgage and bought a new car. But as the reality of his newfound wealth sank in, his spending habits changed dramatically. He purchased a sprawling mansion and filled it with expensive furniture and electronics. Jack bought luxury cars for himself and gifts for friends and family. He invested heavily in his cousin's start-up tech company without proper due diligence. Jack quit his job and began traveling the world, staying at five-star hotels and indulging in lavish experiences. He gambled at high-stakes tables in Las Vegas and Monte Carlo, convinced his luck would hold. But luck is fickle. The tech company failed spectacularly. The real estate market dipped, devaluing his property investments. His gambling losses mounted. Within three years, Jack's fortune had dwindled to almost nothing. Debt collectors called constantly. He was forced to sell his mansion and move back into a small apartment. Five years after his lucky day, Jack found himself applying for his old job at the factory. As he filled out the application, he reflected on how quickly ten million dollars had slipped through his fingers. The lottery had changed his life twice, once with a stroke of luck, and again with a harsh lesson about the fleeting nature of unearned wealth.

Lastly, the instant prosperity myth often overlooks the importance of creating value for others as a path to wealth. Sustainable wealth is frequently built by individuals and businesses that solve problems or fulfill needs for a large number of people.

This value creation takes time, effort, and often multiple iterations to perfect, a process that is fundamentally at odds with the notion of instant riches. An example is David Steward, who is worth approximately $ 11.39 billion dollars. In 1990, he founded World Wide Technology which specializes in technology products and services. Robert F. Smith who is worth $10.8 billion. Mr. Smith has worked with Kraft General Foods and acquired two patents. He worked as an Investment Banker for Goldman Sachs in their Technology Investment Banking division. During his tenure at Goldman Sachs, he advised over $50 billion in merger and acquisition deals for Tech Companies. He later founded Vista Equity Partners which is worth approximately $46 billion in assets. Another notable example is, Sevetri Wilson, founder of Solid Ground Innovations and Resilia. She is a serial entrepreneur, tech founder, wealth creator and change agent. She is also a Writer. Her book is titled, Solid Ground: How I Built a 7-Figure Company at 22 with Zero Capital. Lastly, Janice Bryant Howroyd is a pioneering African American entrepreneur and businesswoman. She is the founder and CEO of ActOne Group, a global enterprise providing workforce solutions, staffing, and human resources services. Founded in 1978, ActOne Group has grown to become the largest privately held, woman-owned workforce solutions company in the United States. Bryant Howroyd is renowned for her innovative leadership and commitment to diversity and inclusion in the workplace. She is also a mentor, author, and motivational speaker, inspiring many with her story of resilience and success. Her accolades include being listed among Forbes' America's Richest Self-Made Women and receiving numerous awards for her contributions to business and community development.

By understanding and dispelling the myth of instant prosperity, individuals can focus on more realistic and sustainable approaches to building wealth. This includes continuous learning, strategic planning, disciplined saving and investing, and a long-term perspective that acknowledges the time and effort required to achieve genuine financial success.

To debunk the myth of instant prosperity, it's essential to understand the true nature of wealth creation. Genuine wealth is typically built over time through a combination of factors: consistent effort, smart financial decisions, strategic investments, and the power of compound interest. It often involves developing valuable skills, creating products or services that provide value to others, and making informed choices about saving and investing. Consider the stories of many self-made millionaires and billionaires. While the media might focus on their current success, a closer look often reveals years or even decades of hard work, failures, and learning experiences that preceded their eventual breakthrough. For example, Amazon founder Jeff Bezos spent years building his company from a small online bookstore to the e-commerce giant it is today. Similarly, Warren Buffett, one of the world's most successful investors, began his journey in finance at a young age and spent decades honing his investment strategies. These stories highlight an important truth: what often appears as "overnight success" is usually the result of years of dedication, learning, and persistent effort. The myth of instant prosperity obscures this reality, leading many to underestimate the time and effort required to achieve significant financial success.

Another aspect of the instant prosperity myth that needs debunking is the idea that wealth alone equates to happiness or fulfillment. While financial security can certainly contribute to well-being, research has consistently shown that beyond a certain point, increases in wealth do not correlate with proportional increases in happiness. This suggests that the pursuit of instant riches as a path to contentment is likely to lead to disappointment. This misconception is deeply ingrained in many societies, often fueled by media portrayals of wealthy individuals living seemingly perfect lives. However, the reality is far more complex. While financial security can certainly contribute to well-being, research has consistently shown that beyond a certain point, increases in wealth do not correlate with proportional increases in happiness. This phenomenon, often referred to as the "hedonic treadmill" or "hedonic adaptation," suggests that humans tend to return to a relatively stable level of happiness despite major positive or negative life changes.

Several studies support this concept:

1. A well-known 2010 study by Daniel Kahneman and Angus Deaton found that emotional well-being rises with income, but only up to an annual income of about $75,000 (adjusted for inflation, this would be higher today). Beyond this point, additional income did not significantly impact day-to-day happiness. It is important to note that this study took place between 2008 and 2009. Initially, the study began with 450,000 people surveyed. However, the results of 14,510 individuals did not meet the criteria for the survey, so the actual number of people surveyed was 435,490.

2. Research published in Nature Human Behavior in 2018 found that the ideal income for life satisfaction in North America is $105,000 per year. Earnings beyond this point were associated with reduced life satisfaction. "That might be surprising as what we see on TV and what advertisers tell us we need would indicate that there is no ceiling when it comes to how much money is needed for happiness, but we now see there are some thresholds," said Andrew T. Jebb, the lead author and doctoral student in the **Department of Psychological Sciences**. "It's been debated at what point does money no longer change your level of well-being. We found that the ideal income point is $95,000 for life evaluation and $60,000 to $75,000 for emotional well-being. Again, this amount is for individuals and would likely be higher for families." The study also found once the threshold was reached, further increases in income tended to be associated with reduced life satisfaction and a lower level of well-being. This may be because money is important for meeting basic needs, purchasing conveniences, and maybe even loan repayments, but to a point. After the optimal point of needs is met, people may be driven by desires such as pursuing more material gains and engaging in social comparisons, which could, ironically, lower well-being.

These findings suggest that the pursuit of instant riches as a path to contentment is likely to lead to disappointment. True fulfillment and happiness are more closely linked to factors such as:

1. Strong social connections and relationships

2. A sense of purpose or meaning in life

3. Personal growth and achievement

4. Physical and mental health

5. Engagement in fulfilling activities or hobbies

6. Contributing to something larger than oneself

The single-minded pursuit of wealth can often come at the expense of these other important aspects of life. Many individuals who achieve significant financial success report feeling isolated, stressed, or unfulfilled if they've neglected other areas of their lives in the process. It's also worth noting that the way wealth is acquired can impact its effect on happiness. Sudden windfalls, such as lottery winnings, often lead to short-term happiness spikes followed by a return to baseline or even decreased life satisfaction. In contrast, wealth accumulated gradually through meaningful work or entrepreneurship may be more likely to contribute to long-term satisfaction. Financial stability is important for well-being, the notion that vast wealth is a guaranteed path to happiness is a myth. A more balanced approach to life satisfaction, one that considers multiple facets of human needs and experiences, is likely to yield more genuine and lasting contentment.

One of the most prevalent manifestations of the instant prosperity myth in modern society is the lottery. Millions of people regularly spend money on lottery tickets, driven by the dream of instant wealth. However, the odds of winning a major lottery jackpot are astronomically low, often in the range of one in hundreds of millions. Despite these odds, the allure of a life-changing windfall keeps people coming back, often spending significant amounts of money over time on what is essentially a losing proposition. Studies of lottery winners reveal that sudden wealth doesn't guarantee long-term financial security or happiness. Many lottery winners struggle to manage their newfound wealth effectively, with some even ending up worse off financially than they were before their win. This phenomenon, sometimes called the "lottery curse," underscores the importance of financial literacy and responsible money management – skills that are often overlooked in the pursuit of instant riches.

The myth of instant prosperity can also manifest in more insidious ways, such as through investment scams and fraudulent financial schemes. For example:

1. Ponzi Schemes: Promoters promise high returns with little or no risk to investors, using new investors' funds to pay returns to earlier investors, creating the illusion of a profitable business.

2. Pump and Dump Schemes: Fraudsters artificially inflate the price of a stock they own through false and misleading positive statements, selling off their shares at the high price, and leaving other investors with worthless stock.

3. Fake Investment Opportunities: Scammers create fake investment opportunities, such as real estate projects or new business ventures, convincing people to invest large sums of money with the promise of quick, substantial returns, only to disappear with the funds.

4. Cryptocurrency Scams: Fraudulent schemes involving cryptocurrencies where scammers lure investors with promises of huge profits through initial coin offerings (ICOs) or trading platforms that later turn out to be fake.

5. High-Yield Investment Programs (HYIPs): These online schemes promise very high returns on investment, often by claiming to invest in forex trading or other high-risk financial instruments, but typically collapse when new investments stop coming in. Promises of extraordinarily high returns with little or

no risk should always be viewed with skepticism. Legitimate investments typically involve a trade-off between risk and reward, and any opportunity that seems too good to be true probably is. Unfortunately, the desire for quick wealth can cloud judgment, making people more susceptible to these types of scams. It's important to recognize that the instant prosperity myth isn't just about money, it can extend to other areas of life as well. We see it in promises of instant weight loss, immediate career success, or perfect relationships without effort.

These ideas all share a common thread: the notion that desirable outcomes can be achieved without the investment of time, effort, and often, some degree of struggle or discomfort.

Debunking the myth of instant prosperity requires a shift in mindset. Instead of focusing on quick wins or overnight success, it's crucial to adopt a long-term perspective on wealth creation. This involves setting realistic financial goals, developing a solid plan to achieve them, and being prepared for the journey to take time and involve challenges along the way. One effective way to counter the allure of instant prosperity is to educate oneself about personal finance and wealth-building strategies. Understanding concepts like compound interest, diversification, and risk management can help individuals make more informed decisions about their money. It also helps to demystify the wealth-creation process, making it clear that while significant financial success is achievable, it typically requires knowledge, strategy, and patience.

Another important aspect of debunking the instant prosperity myth is recognizing the value of incremental progress. Small, consistent steps towards financial goals may not be as exciting as the prospect of sudden riches, but they're far more likely to lead to sustainable wealth over time. This could involve regular savings, gradual debt reduction, or steadily building a diversified investment portfolio. It's also worth considering the role of instant gratification in perpetuating the myth of instant prosperity. Our culture often emphasizes immediate rewards, whether through social media likes, fast food, or on-demand entertainment. This conditioning can make it challenging to embrace the delayed gratification necessary for long-term wealth building. Recognizing this cultural influence and consciously choosing to prioritize long-term benefits over short-term pleasures is an important step in overcoming the instant prosperity myth.

One of the most powerful tools in debunking the myth of instant prosperity is understanding the concept of compound interest. Often called the "eighth wonder of the world" by Albert Einstein (though this attribution is debated), compound interest demonstrates how wealth can grow exponentially over time when returns are reinvested. This principle underlies much of long-term investing and saving strategies, showing how seemingly small, consistent actions can lead to significant wealth accumulation over years or decades. For example, consider two individuals: one who invests $5,000 a year from age 25 to 35 and then stops, and another who starts investing $5,000 a year at age 35 and continues until age 65. Assuming an average annual return of 7%, the first individual who started earlier but invested for only ten years would end up with more money at age 65 than the second individual who invested for 30 years. This illustrates the power of time and compound interest in wealth building, contradicting the notion of instant prosperity.

Another myth that often goes hand in hand with instant prosperity is the idea that wealthy individuals possess some secret knowledge or skill that allows them to accumulate riches quickly. While specialized knowledge can certainly be valuable in certain fields, the reality is that most sustainable wealth is built through well-understood principles: living below one's means, saving consistently, investing wisely, and often, building businesses that provide value to others. It's also important to address the role of luck or chance in wealth creation. While it's true that some individuals benefit from fortunate circumstances, being born into wealth, receiving an unexpected inheritance, or being in the right place at the right time for a business opportunity, relying on luck is not a sound financial strategy. Even in cases where luck plays a role, it's often the preparation and actions of the individual that allow them to capitalize on the opportunity.

The myth of instant prosperity can be particularly dangerous when it intersects with the realities of poverty and economic inequality. For individuals struggling financially, the promise of a quick fix or a way out of their difficulties can be especially alluring. This vulnerability can lead to exploitation, whether through predatory lending practices, multi-level marketing schemes, or other dubious financial propositions that promise fast results but often leave people worse off. Instead of seeking instant solutions, addressing systemic inequalities and providing education and resources for financial literacy can be more effective in creating pathways out of poverty. This approach recognizes that while individual effort is important, broader societal factors also play a significant role in economic outcomes.

It's worth examining how the media and advertising contribute to the perpetuation of the instant prosperity myth. Reality TV shows featuring sudden fame and fortune, advertisements promising quick and easy solutions to complex problems, and news stories that focus on exceptional cases of rapid wealth accumulation all contribute to a skewed perception of how financial success typically occurs. Developing media literacy and the ability to critically evaluate these messages is crucial in resisting the allure of instant prosperity myths.

The rise of social media has added a new dimension to the instant prosperity myth. Carefully curated online personas can give the impression of overnight success, luxurious lifestyles, and effortless wealth. However, these portrayals often mask the realities of hard work, strategic planning, and sometimes, significant debt or financial instability behind the scenes. Recognizing that social media presents a filtered version of reality can help in maintaining a more grounded and realistic perspective on wealth and success.

One effective way to counter the myth of instant prosperity is to focus on the concept of "slow and steady" wealth building. This approach emphasizes consistency, patience, and the power of small actions compounded over time. For instance, the practice of dollar-cost averaging, investing a fixed amount regularly regardless of market conditions, can lead to significant wealth accumulation over the long term, while also reducing the impact of market volatility. Another important aspect of debunking the instant prosperity myth is understanding the role of failure in success. Many of the world's most successful entrepreneurs and investors have experienced significant setbacks and failures on their path to wealth. These experiences, while challenging, often provide valuable lessons and contribute to eventual success. The myth of instant prosperity, with its focus on overnight success, fails to account for the learning and growth that come from overcoming obstacles. It's also crucial to address the psychological impact of believing in instant prosperity. The constant pursuit of a "big break" or a life-changing windfall can lead to chronic dissatisfaction with one's current financial situation. This discontent can manifest as stress, anxiety, and even depression. By contrast, adopting a more realistic view of wealth creation can lead to greater peace of mind and a sense of control over one's financial future. Debunking the myth of instant prosperity also involves redefining what prosperity means. True prosperity goes beyond mere financial wealth to encompass overall well-being, including health, relationships, personal growth, and contribution to society. This broader perspective can help shift focus away from the narrow pursuit of quick riches towards a more holistic and sustainable approach to success.

One of the most insidious aspects of the instant prosperity myth is how it can divert attention and resources away from proven wealth-building strategies. Time and money spent chasing get-rich-quick schemes or high-risk, high-reward investments could often be better used in pursuing education, developing marketable skills, or building a sustainable business. By focusing on these foundational elements, individuals can create a solid base for long-term financial success. It's important to recognize that the myth of instant prosperity often preys on human emotions, particularly fear and greed. Fear of missing out on a supposedly once-in-a-lifetime opportunity can drive people to make hasty and ill-considered financial decisions. Similarly, greed, the desire for more than we need ,can cloud judgment and lead to excessive risk-taking. Developing emotional intelligence and the ability to make rational, rather than emotional, financial decisions is key to avoiding the pitfalls of instant prosperity myths.

Another aspect of debunking the instant prosperity myth involves understanding the role of financial institutions and the broader economic system. While it's true that some individuals and institutions profit from others' pursuit of quick riches (think of casinos or certain types of speculative investments), the overall economic system tends to reward sustained value creation over time. This is why stable, profitable businesses and consistent, long-term investors tend to fare better than those constantly chasing the next big thing. It's also worth considering how the myth of instant prosperity can impact career choices and professional development. The allure of getting rich quickly might lead someone to neglect building a solid career foundation or developing valuable skills in favor of pursuing risky ventures.

However, many of the world's wealthiest individuals built their fortunes on the back of successful careers where they developed expertise and industry knowledge over many years.

One effective strategy for countering the myth of instant prosperity is to focus on financial independence rather than extreme wealth. The concept of financial independence – having enough wealth to live on without active income , is often more achievable and can provide a sense of security and freedom. This shift in focus from "getting rich quick" to "becoming financially secure over time" can lead to more realistic goal-setting and sustainable financial practices. It's also important to address the role of consumer culture in perpetuating the myth of instant prosperity. The constant bombardment of advertisements and societal pressure to own the latest products or live a certain lifestyle can create a sense of lack, fueling the desire for instant wealth. Developing a more mindful approach to consumption and learning to find satisfaction in non-material aspects of life can help resist these pressures and focus on genuine wealth building.

Another key aspect of debunking the instant prosperity myth is understanding the importance of financial planning and professional advice. While the myth often suggests that wealth can be achieved without much thought or planning, the reality is that successful wealth management typically involves careful strategizing, often with the help of financial professionals. Recognizing the value of expert advice and long-term planning is crucial in moving away from the instant prosperity mindset. It's worth noting that while the myth of instant prosperity is harmful, the desire for financial improvement is not inherently negative. The key is to channel this desire into productive, realistic actions rather than chasing unrealistic dreams. Setting achievable financial goals, developing a solid plan to reach them, and celebrating small victories along the way can provide the sense of progress and achievement that many seek from the idea of instant wealth.

As we end our exploration of the instant prosperity myth, it's important to emphasize that debunking this myth is not about discouraging ambition or suggesting that significant financial success is impossible. Rather, it's about promoting a more realistic, sustainable approach to wealth creation that aligns with how financial success is typically achieved in the real world. By understanding the falsehoods inherent in the instant prosperity myth, individuals can make more informed decisions about their financial futures. They can redirect energy from chasing unlikely windfalls towards building the skills, knowledge, and habits that lead to long-term financial security and success. This shift not only increases the likelihood of achieving genuine prosperity but also promotes a healthier relationship with money and a more balanced approach to life. Ultimately, debunking the myth of instant prosperity is about empowerment. It's about taking control of one's financial future rather than leaving it to chance or unrealistic expectations. By embracing the principles of patient wealth building, continuous learning, and perseverance in the face of challenges, individuals can work towards true prosperity, not just in financial terms, but in the broader sense of a life well-lived.

As we move forward, let's carry with us the understanding that real wealth ,both material and otherwise ,is built over time through consistent effort, wise decisions, and a willingness to learn and adapt. By rejecting the false promises of instant prosperity and embracing a more grounded, long-term approach, we open ourselves up to the genuine opportunities for growth and success that exist in the world around us.

Debunking the Myth of Instant Prosperity

Reflective Questions

1. What personal experiences or observations have led you to believe in the concept of instant prosperity?
2. How do you define true financial success, and how does this definition align or conflict with the idea of getting rich quickly?
3. Can you identify any common patterns or characteristics among stories of overnight success? What might be missing from these narratives?
4. How do societal pressures and media portrayals influence your perception of wealth and success?
5. What long-term financial strategies and habits can contribute to sustained prosperity, as opposed to quick gains?
6. Have you ever encountered investment opportunities that seemed too good to be true? What were the red flags, and how did you respond?
7. What role does financial education play in protecting oneself from scams and fraudulent schemes promising instant wealth?
8. How can cultivating patience and a long-term perspective impact your financial decisions and overall well-being?
9. What examples of successful individuals demonstrate the importance of hard work, perseverance, and time in achieving financial success?
10. How can you balance the desire for financial growth with realistic expectations and ethical considerations in your pursuit of prosperity?

Chapter 2:
Challenging Limiting Beliefs About Wealth

When it comes to building wealth, one of the biggest obstacles isn't a lack of opportunity or resources, it's the limiting beliefs that many of us hold about money. These deep-seated beliefs, often ingrained from a young age, can significantly influence our financial decisions and ultimately, our financial success. To transform your financial reality, it's crucial to first identify and then challenge these limiting beliefs. As motivational speaker Tony Robbins says, "The only thing that's keeping you from getting what you want is the story you keep telling yourself." For example, saying to yourself "I don't deserve to be rich" can sabotage your efforts to transform your financial situation. Another example is "It takes money to make money" which can prevent you for taking a step towards starting a business or investing.

The Impact of Limiting Beliefs:

1. Decision paralysis: Fear of making the wrong financial move can lead to inaction.

2. Risk aversion: Overestimating risks can prevent you from making potentially profitable investments.

3. Underearning: Believing you don't deserve more can lead to settling for less in your career.

4. Overspending: If you believe money is evil, you might subconsciously try to get rid of it.

5. Lack of financial education: If you believe you're not smart enough, you might avoid learning about money management.

Challenging and Changing Limiting Beliefs:

1. Awareness: The first step is recognizing your limiting beliefs. Pay attention to your thoughts and reactions regarding money.

2. Question your beliefs: Ask yourself, "Is this belief absolutely true? Where did it come from? How is it serving me?"

3. Seek evidence to the contrary: Look for examples that disprove your limiting beliefs.

4. Reframe negative beliefs: Transform "Money is the root of all evil" to "Money is a tool that can be used for good."

5. Affirmations and visualization: Use positive affirmations and visualize yourself succeeding financially.

6. Educate yourself: Learn about personal finance and wealth-building strategies.

7. Surround yourself with positive influences: Engage with people who have healthy money mindsets.

Creating New, Empowering Beliefs:

1. I have the power to create wealth.

2. Money is a tool for creating positive change.

3. I deserve financial abundance.

4. I am capable of making smart financial decisions.

5. There are always opportunities to increase my wealth.

6. I can start building wealth with what I have right now.

Taking Action:

1. Set clear financial goals aligned with your new beliefs.

2. Create a budget that reflects your values and aspirations.

3. Start investing, even if it's a small amount.

4. Continuously educate yourself about personal finance and wealth-building strategies.

5. Seek mentorship or guidance from financially successful individuals.

6. Practice gratitude for the abundance you already have in your life.

Remember, changing deeply ingrained beliefs is a process that takes time and persistence. Be patient with yourself and celebrate small victories along the way. As you shift your mindset and align your actions with your new beliefs, you'll likely find that your financial reality begins to transform. The key is to remain committed to your personal growth and financial education. By addressing and overcoming these limiting beliefs, you open yourself up to a world of financial possibilities. You'll be more likely to recognize opportunities, take calculated risks, and make decisions that align with your long-term financial goals. Remember, wealth is not just about accumulating money; it's about creating a life of abundance, freedom, and the ability to make a positive impact in the world.

Limiting Belief Examples:

Limiting Belief #1: "Money is the Root of All Evil"

This belief that money is the root of all evil is one of the most pervasive and damaging misconceptions about wealth. Many people grow up hearing this phrase, leading to guilt and discomfort when they start to accumulate wealth. However, this is a misinterpretation of the actual biblical scripture, which states, "For the love of money is a root of all kinds of evil" (1 Timothy 6:10). The key difference lies in how you view and relate to money. Money, in itself, is neutral, it's a tool that can be used for good or evil depending on the intentions behind it. As Benjamin Franklin wisely noted, "Money has never made man happy, nor will it, there is nothing in its nature to produce happiness. The more of it one has the more one wants." This quote highlights that it's not money itself that's problematic, but rather our attitude towards it. By reframing your perspective to see money as a means to create positive change in your life and the lives of others, you can break free from this limiting belief and begin to welcome wealth without guilt. Consider the words of Mahatma Gandhi: "Capital as such is not evil; it is its wrong use that is evil. Capital in some form or other will always be needed." This perspective allows us to separate the tool from its application.

Many successful individuals and philanthropists have demonstrated how wealth can be a force for good. For example, Bill and Melinda Gates have used their vast wealth to tackle global health issues and improve education. Through their foundation, they've contributed billions to causes such as eradicating polio and malaria. Warren Buffett, one of the wealthiest people in the world, pledged to give away 99% of his wealth to philanthropic causes, stating, "If you're in the luckiest 1% of humanity, you owe it to the rest of humanity to think about the other 99%."

Even on a smaller scale, wealth can be used to create positive change. Consider social entrepreneurs like Muhammad Yunus, who used his economic expertise to develop microfinance, providing small loans to help people escape poverty. He once said, "Poverty is not created by poor people. It's created by the system we have built." As the philanthropist Andrew Carnegie once said, "Wealth is not to feed our egos, but to feed the hungry and to help people help themselves." Carnegie, who donated the vast majority of his wealth to establish libraries, schools, and universities, believed that the wealthy had a moral obligation to use their riches for the greater good. By adopting this perspective, you can begin to see wealth not as something inherently evil, but as a powerful tool for positive change. This shift in mindset allows you to pursue financial success without moral conflict, knowing that your wealth can be a force for good in the world. As you accumulate wealth, you can ask yourself, "How can I use this to improve my life and the lives of others?" This approach aligns your financial goals with your values, creating a harmonious and purposeful pursuit of prosperity.

Limiting Belief #2: "I Don't Deserve to Be Wealthy"

Another common belief is that wealth is reserved for a select few, those who are smarter, more talented, or simply luckier. This belief can stem from feelings of inadequacy or a lack of self-worth, leading to self-sabotaging behaviors. Warren Buffett, one of the world's most successful investors, challenges this notion by stating, "I am not the smartest, but I am very good at controlling my emotions." This quote underscores that success in wealth-building isn't solely about intelligence, but also about emotional intelligence and discipline. The idea that wealth is a limited resource can be particularly damaging. It creates a scarcity mindset that can lead to fear-based decision-making and missed opportunities. However, wealth is not a zero-sum game; there's enough for everyone. This concept is beautifully illustrated by the story of Andrew Carnegie, who started as a poor immigrant and became one of the wealthiest men in history. Carnegie famously said, "The first man gets the oyster, the second man gets the shell." His point was that there are always opportunities for those who are willing to look for them and work hard. Successful people often aren't the smartest or the luckiest, they are those who believe they deserve success and take consistent action towards it. Take the example of Sara Blakely, the founder of Spanx. Blakely wasn't born into wealth or privilege, nor did she have any special connections in the fashion industry. What she did have was a belief in herself and her product. She once said, "Don't be intimidated by what you don't know. That can be your greatest strength and ensure that you do things differently from everyone else." This mindset led her to become the youngest self-made female billionaire in America. To overcome this belief, start by affirming your worthiness. As Oprah Winfrey, one of the world's most successful women, says, "You deserve the best that life has to offer." Embrace this truth, and remind yourself daily that you are deserving of financial abundance. This shift in mindset can be transformative. Take the case of Chris Gardner, whose story was portrayed in the film "The Pursuit of Happiness." Despite facing homelessness and single parenthood, Gardner's belief in his own potential led him to persevere and eventually become a multimillionaire stockbroker. It's also crucial to understand that wealth creation is often a gradual process.

Finally, remember that your current circumstances do not dictate your future potential. Jim Carrey, the famous actor, once wrote himself a check for $10 million for "acting services rendered," dated it 10 years in the future, and kept it in his wallet. Before the 10 years were up, he found out he was going to make $10 million for his role in "Dumb and Dumber." This story exemplifies the power of belief and visualization in achieving financial success.

By challenging the belief that wealth is only for a select few, you open yourself up to a world of possibilities. As you begin to see wealth as accessible and deserved, you're more likely to take the necessary steps to achieve it. Remember, as the famous saying goes, "Whether you think you can, or you think you can't, you're right." Your beliefs shape your reality, so choose beliefs that empower you towards financial success.

Limiting Belief #3: "You Have to Work Extremely Hard to Be Wealthy"

While hard work is certainly a component of success, the belief that you must work endlessly to achieve wealth can lead to burnout and resentment. Many people equate wealth with endless struggle, but this doesn't have to be the case. The key is to work smarter, not harder. This sentiment is echoed by Tim Ferriss, author of "The 4-Hour Work Week," who argues, "Focus on being productive instead of busy." Ferriss's own journey from overworked entrepreneur to successful investor and author exemplifies this principle. He emphasizes the importance of prioritizing high-impact activities and eliminating time-wasters, a strategy that has allowed him to build wealth while maintaining a balanced lifestyle. Leverage your skills, invest in assets that generate passive income, and build systems that allow your money to work for you. Robert Kiyosaki, in his book "Rich Dad Poor Dad," introduces the concept of assets versus liabilities, stating, "The rich buy assets. The poor only have expenses. The middle class buy liabilities they think are assets." This perspective shift can be transformative. For instance, consider the story of Pat Flynn, who lost his job in 2008 but turned his misfortune into opportunity by creating Smart Passive Income, a blog and podcast that now generates substantial passive income through affiliate marketing and digital products. Warren Buffett, one of the wealthiest individuals in the world, emphasizes the importance of investing wisely rather than working harder. He states, "If you don't find a way to make money while you sleep, you will work until you die." This philosophy is reflected in Buffett's investment strategy, which focuses on buying undervalued companies and holding them for the long term, allowing compound interest to work its magic. Another example is Jeff Bezos, who built Amazon on the principle of scalability. Bezos once said, "I very frequently get the question: 'What's going to change in the next 10 years?' And that is a very interesting question; it's a very common one. I almost never get the question: 'What's not going to change in the next 10 years?' And I submit to you that that second question is actually the more important of the two." By focusing on creating systems and infrastructure that could grow exponentially, Bezos was able to build one of the world's most valuable companies.

By shifting your focus from effort to strategy, you can challenge this limiting belief and open the door to greater financial freedom. This doesn't mean abandoning hard work altogether, but rather being strategic about where you direct your efforts. For example, real estate mogul Barbara Corcoran started her empire with a $1,000 loan and built it into a multi-million-dollar business. She advises, "The difference between successful people and others is how long they spend time feeling sorry for themselves." Corcoran's success came not just from working hard, but from strategically reinvesting her profits and building a brand that could grow beyond her personal efforts. Remember, the goal is not to work yourself to exhaustion, but to create a life of abundance and freedom. As entrepreneur and motivational speaker Jim Rohn put it, "Profits are better than wages. Wages make you a living; profits make you a fortune." By focusing on building assets, creating systems, and making strategic investments, you can break free from the belief that endless toil is the only path to wealth. Instead, you can create a life where your money works for you, allowing you to enjoy the fruits of your labor and pursue the things that truly matter to you.

Limiting Belief #4: "Rich People Are Greedy and Corrupt"

The belief that money is inherently evil or that wealthy people are inherently greedy or unethical can create a powerful negative association with wealth, causing you to unconsciously repel financial success. This limiting belief often stems from cultural narratives, personal experiences, or misinterpretations of sayings like "money is the root of all evil" (which is actually a misquote - the original states "the love of money is the root of all evil"). However, the idea that all wealthy people are greedy or unethical is simply not true. As Warren Buffett, known for his frugal lifestyle despite his immense wealth, once said, "If you're in the luckiest 1% of humanity, you owe it to the rest of humanity to think about the other 99%." This quote exemplifies how wealth can be viewed as a responsibility rather than a tool for personal gain. Many affluent individuals use their wealth to make significant contributions to society. For instance, philanthropists like Bill Gates and Melinda French Gates have donated billions to global health initiatives, education, and poverty alleviation through their foundation. Bill Gates has stated, "Success is a lousy teacher. It seduces smart people into thinking they can't lose." This mindset has driven him to use his wealth to tackle some of the world's most pressing problems. Another example is Mackenzie Scott, who has given away billions of dollars to various causes and non-profits. She once wrote, "There's no question in my mind that anyone's personal wealth is the product of a collective effort, and of social structures which present opportunities to some people, and obstacles to countless others." This perspective reframes wealth as a means to give back to the society that made it possible.

By recognizing that wealth can be a powerful tool for good, you can shift your mindset from associating money with greed to seeing it as an opportunity to make a positive impact. Take the case of Chuck Feeney, co-founder of Duty-Free Shoppers Group. Feeney secretly gave away his entire $8 billion fortune to various charitable causes over his lifetime. His philosophy? "I had one idea that never changed in my mind, that you should use your wealth to help people." This example shows that wealth and generosity are not mutually exclusive, but can in fact be deeply intertwined. It's also important to recognize that ethical wealth creation can have positive ripple effects throughout society. Consider the story of Hamdi Ulukaya, founder of Chobani yogurt. Not only did Ulukaya build a successful business, but he also implemented progressive policies like offering shares to employees and hiring refugees. He once said, "The minute a refugee has a job, that's the minute they stop being a refugee." This demonstrates how ethical business practices can create wealth not just for the owner, but for employees and communities as well.

Shifting this mindset doesn't mean you have to become a billionaire philanthropist overnight. It starts with recognizing that money itself is neutral, it's how it's used that matters. As Oprah Winfrey put it, "The reason I've been able to be so financially successful is my focus has never, ever for one minute been money." By focusing on creating value, solving problems, and making a positive impact, you can align your pursuit of wealth with your values and ethics. This shift can not only remove a significant mental block to your financial success but also inspire you to use whatever wealth you accumulate in ways that align with your deepest values and aspirations for a better world.

Limiting Belief #5: "I Will Never Be Good with Money"

If you believe that you're inherently bad with money, you're likely to fulfill that prophecy. This belief often stems from past financial mistakes or a lack of financial education. However, financial literacy is a skill that anyone can learn and improve over time. Just because you've made mistakes in the past doesn't mean you're doomed to repeat them. This sentiment is echoed by Tony Robbins, who states, "The path to success is to take massive, determined action." Robbins himself went from living in a 400-square-foot apartment and washing dishes in the bathtub to becoming a multimillionaire through his commitment to personal growth and financial education. Take control of your financial education, seek out resources, and learn from your experiences. The journey to financial literacy can start small and grow over time. Warren Buffett, one of the most successful investors in history, emphasizes the importance of continuous learning: "The more you learn, the more you earn." Buffett's own story is a testament to this philosophy. He bought his first stock at age 11 and has been constantly educating himself about business and finance ever since, leading to his extraordinary success.

It's crucial to understand that financial mistakes are not permanent character flaws, but opportunities for growth. Take the example of Mark Cuban, who went from sleeping on the floor of a shared apartment to becoming a billionaire. Cuban has been open about his early financial struggles and mistakes, saying, "It doesn't matter how many times you fail. You only have to be right once and then everyone can tell you that you are an overnight success." His story illustrates that financial success is often built on a foundation of lessons learned from past mistakes. By adopting a growth mindset and committing to learning, you can overcome this limiting belief and take charge of your financial future. This approach is exemplified by Ray Dalio, founder of Bridgewater Associates, who advocates for "radical transparency" in facing one's mistakes and weaknesses. Dalio argues, "Pain plus reflection equals progress." This philosophy has guided him in building one of the world's largest hedge funds, despite early career setbacks. Remember, financial literacy is not an innate trait but a learned skill. Just as you would approach learning a new language or sport, approach your financial education with patience and persistence. Suze Orman, a renowned personal finance expert, often says, "When it comes to money, knowledge is power." Start by understanding basic concepts like budgeting, saving, and investing, and gradually build your knowledge over time.

Lastly, it's important to surround yourself with resources and people who support your financial growth. Seek out mentors, join financial education groups, or enroll in courses. As motivational speaker Jim Rohn famously said, "You are the average of the five people you spend the most time with." By surrounding yourself with financially literate individuals and resources, you create an environment conducive to your own financial growth and success.

Limiting Belief #6 "There's never enough to go around."

This scarcity mindset can lead to hoarding behavior and missed opportunities. When we believe resources are limited, we tend to cling tightly to what we have, fearing loss and overlooking potential gains. This mindset can manifest in various ways, from keeping money in low-yield savings accounts instead of investing, to refusing potentially lucrative partnerships out of fear of competition. In contrast, adopting an abundance mindset opens up possibilities for growth and collaboration. This perspective recognizes that wealth and opportunities are not finite - they can be created and expanded. An abundance mindset encourages innovation, risk-taking, and mutually beneficial partnerships. Consider the rise of the sharing economy, where companies like Airbnb have created wealth by tapping into existing resources. Airbnb's founders didn't create new hotels or vacation properties. Instead, they recognized the abundance of underutilized living spaces and developed a platform to connect homeowners with travelers. This innovative approach has not only generated significant wealth for the company and many of its users but has also expanded the entire hospitality market. Ride-sharing companies like Uber and Lyft exemplify the abundance mindset. They didn't add more cars to the road; they utilized existing vehicles and drivers' free time to create a new transportation paradigm. This approach has created jobs, improved urban mobility, and generated substantial wealth. Even in traditional industries, an abundance mindset can lead to breakthrough innovations. Tesla, for instance, didn't view the automotive market as saturated. Instead, they saw abundant opportunities in reimagining the car as an electric, software-driven vehicle. This perspective allowed them to disrupt an established industry and create enormous value. Embracing an abundance mindset doesn't mean ignoring real-world constraints or being recklessly optimistic. Rather, it's about approaching challenges with creativity and openness, seeking win-win solutions, and recognizing that value can often be created by reimagining existing resources or systems. By shifting from a scarcity mindset to an abundance mindset, we can unlock new avenues for wealth creation, foster innovation, and contribute to economic growth that benefits not just ourselves, but society as a whole. This shift is a crucial component of the prosperity mindset, enabling us to see and seize opportunities that others might overlook.

List of Limiting Beliefs About Wealth:

1. Money is the root of all evil.

2. I don't deserve to be wealthy.

3. You have to work extremely hard to be wealthy.

4. Rich people are greedy and corrupt.

5. I will never be good with money.

6. Wealth will change who I am.

7. I can't be spiritual and wealthy at the same time.

8. Money can't buy happiness.

9. I have to sacrifice my health and relationships to be rich.

10. It's too late for me to become wealthy.

11. I'm not smart enough to be wealthy.

12. I need to win the lottery to be financially free.

13. It's selfish to want more money.

14. There are no opportunities left to make money.

Challenging these limiting beliefs is the first step towards transforming your financial mindset and, in turn, your financial reality. By replacing these outdated narratives with empowering beliefs, you can pave the way for true prosperity.

Chapter 2: Challenging Limiting Beliefs

Reflective Questions

1. What are the primary limiting beliefs about money and wealth that you've identified in yourself? How have these beliefs impacted your financial decisions and overall financial health?

2. Can you trace the origins of your limiting beliefs about money? Are they rooted in childhood experiences, cultural influences, or past financial setbacks?

3. How might your financial situation be different if you didn't hold these limiting beliefs? Try to envision a scenario where these beliefs don't exist.

4. Which limiting belief do you find most challenging to overcome? What makes this belief particularly persistent or difficult to change?

5. Have you ever challenged a limiting belief about money in the past? What was the outcome, and what did you learn from that experience?

6. How do your current financial habits and decisions reflect your limiting beliefs? Can you identify specific actions or inactions that stem from these beliefs?

7. What evidence can you find in your life or in the lives of others that contradicts your limiting beliefs about money and wealth?

8. If you were to replace your limiting beliefs with empowering ones, what would those new beliefs be? How might they change your approach to personal finance?

9. What steps can you take to actively challenge and reframe your limiting beliefs about money? Consider both mental exercises and practical actions.

10. How might overcoming your limiting beliefs about money impact other areas of your life, such as your career, relationships, or personal growth?

Chapter 3:
Mindset Matters

The journey to building wealth is not merely a matter of financial strategies and market knowledge; it begins in the mind. The mindset with which one approaches wealth creation can be the deciding factor between success and stagnation. A prosperity mindset, one that is open, resilient, and growth-oriented, acts as the cornerstone for all other wealth-building activities. As noted by Napoleon Hill, "Whatever the mind can conceive and believe, it can achieve." This belief underscores the importance of mental and emotional preparedness in the pursuit of financial goals. Building wealth starts by recognizing the power of one's thoughts, attitudes, and beliefs about money, which aligns with the biblical principle found in Proverbs 23:7, "For as he thinks in his heart, so is he."

One of the most critical aspects of the wealth-building mindset is the power of positive thinking. Positive thinking is not about ignoring challenges but about approaching them with the belief that solutions exist and can be found. This mindset fosters creativity, innovation, and perseverance, qualities that are essential for financial success. Consider the story of Oprah Winfrey, who overcame significant obstacles to become one of the wealthiest and most influential women in the world. Her success is often attributed to her unwavering belief in her potential and her refusal to be defined by her circumstances. Oprah once said, "The greatest discovery of all time is that a person can change their future by merely changing their attitude." This quote encapsulates the essence of a wealth-building mindset: the belief that one's thoughts and attitudes can shape their financial destiny, much like the guidance given in Deuteronomy 30:19, which encourages choosing life and blessings through the right mindset and actions.

A prosperity mindset also emphasizes the importance of financial education. Knowledge is power, and in the realm of wealth creation, it is an indispensable tool. The more one understands about money, how it works, how it can be invested, and how it can grow, the more equipped they are to make informed financial decisions. Jim Rohn, a renowned entrepreneur and motivational speaker, stated, "Formal education will make you a living; self-education will make you a fortune." This quote highlights the value of ongoing self-education in the pursuit of wealth. Financial literacy enables individuals to navigate the complexities of the financial world, from understanding the stock market to managing taxes and leveraging investments. It empowers them to seize opportunities and avoid pitfalls that can hinder their progress toward financial independence, which aligns with the wisdom found in Proverbs 24:3-4, "By wisdom a house is built, and through understanding it is established; through knowledge its rooms are filled with rare and beautiful treasures."

Fear is one of the most significant barriers to wealth creation. It can manifest as a fear of failure, fear of loss, or even fear of success. This fear often leads to inaction, preventing individuals from taking the necessary steps to grow their wealth. As Warren Buffett famously stated, "Be fearful when others are greedy and greedy when others are fearful." This quote encapsulates the idea that overcoming fear can lead to significant financial opportunities. However, a prosperity mindset encourages individuals to face their fears and embrace calculated risks. This approach is exemplified by Sara Blakely, founder of Spanx, who overcame her fear of failure by redefining it. She once said, "I feel like failure is life's way of nudging you and letting you know your off course." Blakely's ability to view failure as a learning opportunity rather than a setback was instrumental in her journey to becoming the youngest self-made female billionaire in America. T. Harv Eker, author of "Secrets of the Millionaire Mind," suggests, "If you are willing to do only what's easy, life will be hard. But if you're willing to do what's hard, life will be easy." This mindset shift is crucial for those looking to build wealth. It involves recognizing that risk is an inherent part of the financial landscape and that avoiding it altogether can lead to missed opportunities. Richard Branson, founder of the Virgin Group, embodies this principle. He once stated, "You don't learn to walk by following rules. You learn by doing, and by falling over." Branson's willingness to take calculated risks has led to the creation of over 400 companies under the Virgin brand. Instead, individuals with a prosperity mindset approach risk with caution and preparation, using it as a tool for growth rather than a source of anxiety. This approach is similar to the encouragement found in Isaiah 41:10, "So do not fear, for I am with you; do not be dismayed, for I am your God. I will strengthen you and help you; I will uphold you with my righteous right hand." This biblical verse encourages facing challenges with confidence, much like how successful investors approach market volatility.

Overcoming fear often involves starting small and gradually building confidence. Consider the story of John Paul DeJoria, co-founder of Paul Mitchell hair products and Patrón tequila. DeJoria started his first business while living in his car, overcoming the fear of homelessness to build multiple billion-dollar brands. He often says, "In the end, everything will be okay. If it's not okay, it's not the end." This mindset helped him persevere through numerous setbacks and failures. Another example of overcoming fear in wealth creation is the story of Ray Kroc, who founded McDonald's at the age of 52. Despite initial fears and setbacks, Kroc persevered, famously stating, "If you're not a risk taker, you should get the hell out of business." His willingness to face his fears and take calculated risks transformed a small hamburger stand into a global fast-food empire. It's also important to recognize that fear can sometimes be a useful tool when properly managed. As Mark Cuban, billionaire entrepreneur and investor, puts it, "The only way you're going to get better is to get out there and screw it up over and over again." This perspective reframes fear as an opportunity for growth and learning, rather than a paralyzing force.

Overcoming fear is a crucial step in developing a prosperity mindset and building wealth. By reframing failure as a learning opportunity, taking calculated risks, and gradually building confidence through small steps, individuals can transform their relationship with fear from a barrier to a catalyst for financial growth. As Nelson Mandela once said, "I learned that courage was not the absence of fear, but the triumph over it." This triumph over fear is often the first step on the path to financial success.

Goal-setting is another fundamental component of the wealth-building mindset. Without clear, well-defined goals, financial aspirations remain abstract and unattainable. A prosperity mindset involves setting specific, measurable, achievable, relevant, and time-bound (SMART) goals that provide direction and motivation. Brian Tracy, a motivational speaker and author, once said, "Goals are the fuel in the furnace of achievement." This quote illustrates the driving force that goals provide in the pursuit of wealth. For instance, consider the goal of saving for retirement. Rather than simply deciding to save more money, a SMART goal would specify the amount, timeline, and method. An example might be: "Save $500,000 for retirement by contributing $500 monthly to a retirement account over the next 30 years." This goal is specific in terms of the amount, measurable through monthly contributions, achievable based on income, relevant to long-term financial security, and time-bound with a clear deadline. By setting such detailed goals, individuals create a roadmap for their financial journey, ensuring that each step is purposeful and aligned with their ultimate objectives. Another example is purchasing a home. Instead of vaguely aiming to buy a house someday, a more effective goal could be: "Save $50,000 for a down payment on a home within the next five years by setting aside $10,000 annually." This goal breaks down the larger financial aspiration into manageable steps, making it easier to track progress and stay motivated. The clarity of this goal allows for regular assessment and adjustment, ensuring that the individual remains on course to achieve their dream of homeownership.

Starting a business also benefits from time-based goals. A prospective entrepreneur might set a goal like: "Launch a small business within the next 12 months, with a business plan completed in the first three months, securing funding by month six, and opening by month twelve." This approach divides a complex endeavor into actionable steps, providing both a timeline and a structure to follow. The specificity of the deadlines helps to keep the process moving forward, reducing the likelihood of procrastination or drift. These goals serve as benchmarks for success, helping to measure progress and make necessary adjustments along the way. This principle of goal-setting is reflected in Habakkuk 2:2, "Write the vision and make it plain on tablets, that he may run who reads it." Just as the verse emphasizes the importance of clarity and communication in a vision, setting clear, time-bound goals ensures that individuals remain focused and motivated in their wealth-building efforts. The act of writing down these goals and revisiting them regularly also reinforces commitment and accountability, further enhancing the likelihood of success.

The path to wealth is rarely a smooth one. It is often marked by challenges, setbacks, and unexpected obstacles that test one's resolve. However, those with a prosperity mindset understand that resilience is key to overcoming these hurdles. Resilience, in the context of wealth building, is about the ability to recover quickly from difficulties, to persist in the face of adversity, and to maintain a positive outlook despite setbacks. A prime example of resilience can be seen in the life of Walt Disney. Before becoming one of the most successful entrepreneurs in history, Disney faced numerous failures, including bankruptcy and the loss of his first successful character, Oswald the Lucky Rabbit. Despite these setbacks, Disney persisted, creating Mickey Mouse and eventually building a media empire. Disney's journey was far from easy, but his resilience allowed him to turn obstacles into opportunities. As he once said, "All the adversity I've had in my life, all my troubles and obstacles, have strengthened me... You may not realize it when it happens, but a kick in the teeth may be the best thing in the world for you."

Resilient individuals view setbacks not as failures but as opportunities to learn and grow. This perspective is crucial in wealth building, where challenges such as market downturns, investment losses, or business failures are inevitable. Thomas Edison famously said, "I have not failed. I've just found 10,000 ways that won't work." This quote embodies the resilience required to build wealth. Edison's persistence, despite countless setbacks, ultimately led to the invention of the light bulb, a symbol of enduring success after repeated failure. In the same way, those pursuing wealth must maintain a long-term perspective, staying committed to their financial goals even when the road is rocky. Consider the example of an investor who experiences significant losses during a stock market crash. While the immediate reaction might be one of panic, a resilient mindset would focus on the long-term strategy, recognizing that market volatility is part of the investment journey. Instead of selling off assets in fear, a resilient investor might see the downturn as an opportunity to buy undervalued stocks, confident in the market's eventual recovery. This ability to stay calm and make strategic decisions in the face of adversity is what sets successful investors apart.

Resilience also involves adapting to changing circumstances. In today's fast-paced world, economic conditions, technologies, and industries are constantly evolving. Those with a prosperity mindset are not rigid in their approach but are willing to pivot and adjust their strategies as needed. An example of this adaptability can be seen in the rise of companies like Netflix, which started as a DVD rental service and successfully transitioned to a streaming platform, thriving in a rapidly changing market. By being resilient and adaptable, individuals and businesses can turn potential setbacks into springboards for growth. Resilience is about bouncing back from losses and continuing to move forward. As author and motivational speaker Zig Ziglar said, "It's not how far you fall, but how high you bounce that counts." This quote highlights the importance of resilience in the wealth-building journey. Whether it's recovering from a failed business venture or rebounding after a financial setback, the ability to rise again and continue pursuing one's goals is crucial. This resilience is reflected in the biblical principle of perseverance described in Galatians 6:9, "Let us not become weary in doing good, for at the proper time we will reap a harvest if we do not give up." Just as this verse encourages steadfastness in good deeds, it also speaks to the importance of persistence in the pursuit of wealth. The journey may be long and challenging, but with resilience, the eventual rewards can be significant. Building wealth requires more than just financial acumen; it demands resilience. The ability to learn from setbacks, adapt to new circumstances, and maintain a long-term perspective is what enables individuals to navigate the inevitable challenges along the way. By cultivating resilience, one can transform obstacles into opportunities and continue moving forward on the path to financial success.

Delayed gratification is a concept that lies at the heart of the wealth-building mindset. It involves prioritizing long-term financial goals over immediate desires, a practice that requires both discipline and foresight. By resisting the temptation to indulge in short-term pleasures, individuals can focus on accumulating wealth that will benefit them in the future. For example, consider someone who chooses to drive a modest car and live in a smaller home while investing the money they save into a retirement account or a growing business. This individual understands that by delaying the gratification of purchasing luxury items, they are positioning themselves for greater financial stability and freedom later in life. The decision to forgo an expensive vacation or a designer wardrobe in favor of contributing to a 401(k) or investing in the stock market is a practical application of delayed gratification. Over time, these choices compound, leading to significant financial growth. Zig Ziglar, a motivational speaker, succinctly captured this mindset when he said, "Rich people have small TVs and big libraries, and poor people have small libraries and big TVs." This quote underscores the importance of investing in one's future through education, personal development, and sound financial decisions, rather than indulging in immediate entertainment or luxury. The idea is that wealth is built by prioritizing assets that appreciate in value, like knowledge and investments, over those that offer only fleeting pleasure.

This principle of delayed gratification is not only a modern financial strategy but also has deep roots in ancient wisdom. Proverbs 21:20 states, "The wise store up choice food and olive oil, but fools gulp theirs down," emphasizing the importance of wise stewardship and planning for the future. The verse illustrates the stark contrast between those who prepare for the future and those who consume all they have without thought of tomorrow. By practicing delayed gratification, individuals embody the wisdom of storing up resources for times of need, ensuring long-term security and prosperity. Another practical example is the story of Warren Buffett, one of the most successful investors in history. Buffett is known for his frugal lifestyle and commitment to long-term investing. Even as a billionaire, he famously lives in the same house he purchased in 1958 for $31,500. Buffett's ability to delay gratification and invest in opportunities that yield substantial returns over time has been a key factor in his immense wealth. His approach teaches that wealth-building is not about how much money you make, but how much you save and invest wisely. In contrast, the culture of instant gratification often leads to financial instability. Consider the common scenario of credit card debt, where individuals purchase items, they cannot afford with the promise of paying later. This behavior often results in high-interest debt that erodes wealth rather than builds it. By practicing delayed gratification, individuals can avoid the trap of debt and instead, use their resources to generate future wealth.

The discipline of delayed gratification also fosters a sense of empowerment and control over one's financial destiny. When individuals make conscious choices to save and invest rather than spend impulsively, they take charge of their financial future. This control is empowering, as it shifts the focus from immediate wants to long-term financial well-being. Delayed gratification is a critical element of the wealth-building mindset. By prioritizing long-term financial goals over short-term desires, individuals can accumulate wealth, achieve financial freedom, and enjoy the benefits of their discipline. Whether it's through careful saving, strategic investing, or frugal living, the practice of delayed gratification lays a strong foundation for lasting financial success. This principle, echoed in both modern wisdom and ancient scripture, reminds us that the path to wealth is paved with patience, foresight, and wise choices.

Gratitude is often overlooked in discussions about wealth, but it plays a vital role in fostering a prosperity mindset. A mindset rooted in gratitude shifts the focus from what is lacking to what is already present, creating a foundation for a positive and proactive approach to building wealth. This shift in perspective not only reduces stress and anxiety but also opens the door to greater opportunities. When individuals appreciate what they have, they are more likely to make thoughtful, intentional decisions with their money. For instance, someone who is grateful for their stable income and modest home may be more inclined to invest in their future rather than spending impulsively. This appreciation for what is already in hand fosters a sense of contentment that curbs the urge to seek immediate gratification through unnecessary purchases. As Brian Tracy advises, "Develop an attitude of gratitude, and give thanks for everything that happens to you, knowing that every step forward is a step toward achieving something bigger and better than your current situation."

Gratitude also nurtures a sense of abundance, which is crucial in the wealth-building journey. When people focus on what they have rather than what they lack, they cultivate a mindset that attracts more positive outcomes. For example, a business owner who is thankful for each client, no matter how small the transaction, is likely to provide better service, which in turn can lead to repeat business and referrals. This proactive and appreciative attitude can be the difference between a business that stagnates and one that thrives. Incorporating gratitude into daily life can be as simple as reflecting on the blessings that one might otherwise take for granted. Gratitude affirmations, such as "I am grateful for the financial opportunities that come my way," or "I appreciate the stability and security I have built," can reinforce a wealth-oriented mindset. These affirmations serve as reminders to focus on growth and potential, rather than scarcity and limitations.

Consider the story of Oprah Winfrey, who has often spoken about the power of gratitude in her life. Despite her humble beginnings, Oprah has always maintained a deep sense of gratitude for every opportunity, big or small. This mindset not only helped her to overcome numerous obstacles but also played a key role in her journey to becoming one of the wealthiest and most influential women in the world. Oprah's example illustrates how gratitude can transform challenges into stepping stones toward success. A grateful mindset encourages mindful spending and saving habits. When individuals are thankful for their resources, they tend to manage them more wisely. For example, a person who is grateful for their job might be more diligent in budgeting and saving, recognizing that their income is a valuable tool for future wealth building. This approach contrasts sharply with a mindset of scarcity, which often leads to reckless spending out of fear or a sense of lack. In the biblical context, gratitude is repeatedly emphasized as a key to living a fulfilled and prosperous life. Psalm 100:4 urges, "Enter his gates with thanksgiving and his courts with praise; give thanks to him and praise his name." This verse not only highlights the importance of gratitude in spiritual practice but also suggests that a thankful heart is a pathway to greater blessings. By entering each day with gratitude, individuals align themselves with the principles of abundance and prosperity.

Gratitude Affirmations:

1. "I am thankful for the financial wisdom I have gained."

2. "I appreciate the opportunities to grow my wealth."

3. "I am grateful for the abundance that flows into my life."

4. "I give thanks for the lessons learned through financial challenges."

5. "I am thankful for the resources I have to build a secure future."

6. "I appreciate the support and guidance I receive in my financial journey."

The Prosperity Mindset

7. "I am grateful for the financial stability I am creating."

8. "I give thanks for the opportunities to invest in my future."

9. "I am thankful for the wealth that is growing in my life."

10. "I appreciate every step I take toward financial freedom."

Gratitude is a powerful tool in the wealth-building arsenal. By focusing on what is already present and expressing appreciation for it, individuals cultivate a mindset of abundance and proactive growth. This perspective not only enhances financial decision-making but also attracts further opportunities for prosperity. As individuals practice gratitude daily, they align themselves with the principles of wealth-building, ensuring a more positive and successful financial journey.

Building wealth is not just about individual effort; it also involves cultivating a network of supportive and like-minded individuals. Networking and relationship building are crucial elements of the prosperity mindset. By surrounding oneself with successful, positive, and knowledgeable people, individuals can gain valuable insights, opportunities, and support in their wealth-building journey. Author and entrepreneur Jim Rohn famously said, "You are the average of the five people you spend the most time with." This quote emphasizes the impact that one's social circle can have on their financial success. Building relationships with mentors, peers, and industry professionals can provide the guidance and resources needed to navigate the financial landscape and achieve wealth, a principle that resonates with Proverbs 13:20, "Walk with the wise and become wise, for a companion of fools suffers harm."

A core strategy embraced by those with a prosperity mindset is the creation of multiple income streams. Relying solely on a single source of income can be precarious, leaving individuals vulnerable to economic downturns, job loss, or other unforeseen circumstances. By diversifying income sources, whether through investments, side businesses, or passive income opportunities, individuals can enhance their financial stability and accelerate wealth accumulation. For instance, consider an individual who has a full-time job but also invests in real estate, runs an online business, and earns dividends from stocks. By having multiple income streams, this person is not solely dependent on their job for financial security. If one income stream falters, the others can provide support, reducing overall financial risk. This approach to income diversification not only provides a safety net but also offers greater potential for wealth growth over time. A well-known advocate of income diversification is Warren Buffett. Although Buffett is primarily recognized for his investments, he also emphasizes the importance of multiple income streams.

Buffett famously said, "Never depend on a single income. Make investment to create a second source." This quote encapsulates the philosophy of creating additional streams of income to build a more secure and prosperous financial future.

The principle of income diversification is also rooted in ancient wisdom. Ecclesiastes 11:2 advises, "Invest in seven ventures, yes, in eight; you do not know what disaster may come upon the land." This verse highlights the importance of spreading risk across different ventures, a timeless strategy that remains relevant in today's financial landscape. By diversifying investments and income sources, individuals can protect themselves from unforeseen events that could jeopardize their financial well-being. Creating multiple income streams involves exploring various opportunities that align with one's skills, interests, and financial goals.

Here is a list of potential income streams to consider:

1. Real Estate Investments: Purchasing rental properties, flipping houses, or investing in Real Estate Investment Trusts (REITs).

2. Stock Market Investments: Earning dividends from stocks, investing in mutual funds, or trading options.

3. Side Business or Freelancing: Offering consulting services, freelance writing, graphic design, or other skills-based services.

4. Online Businesses: Launching an e-commerce store, selling digital products, or creating a subscription-based service.

5. Royalties from Intellectual Property: Earning royalties from books, music, patents, or other creative works.

6. Affiliate Marketing: Promoting products or services online and earning a commission on sales generated through your referrals.

7. Peer-to-Peer Lending: Investing in peer-to-peer lending platforms where you earn interest by lending money to individuals or businesses.

8. Content Creation: Monetizing a YouTube channel, podcast, or blog through ads, sponsorships, or product sales.

9. Automated Online Courses: Creating and selling online courses that generate income with minimal ongoing effort.

10. Passive Income through Investments: Investing in bonds, certificates of deposit (CDs), or high-yield savings accounts that generate interest over time.

The diversity of income streams is not only financially beneficial but also encourages a mindset of innovation and continuous learning. When individuals actively seek out new ways to generate income, they often acquire new skills and knowledge, which can further enhance their earning potential. For instance, someone who starts a side business may learn valuable entrepreneurial skills that can be applied to other ventures, leading to even greater income opportunities. This proactive approach to wealth building is essential in a rapidly changing economy, where traditional jobs may no longer provide the security they once did. By diversifying income sources, individuals can adapt to changing economic conditions and remain financially resilient. This mindset aligns with the wisdom of seeking out opportunities and being open to new possibilities, a principle that is key to long-term financial success. Multiple income streams can also lead to the creation of passive income, which is income earned with little to no effort once the initial work has been done. Examples include rental income, royalties from intellectual property, or earnings from investments. Passive income is particularly valuable because it allows individuals to continue generating wealth even when they are not actively working. This can lead to greater financial freedom and the ability to focus on other important aspects of life, such as family, personal development, or philanthropy.

The creation of multiple income streams is a powerful strategy for building wealth and achieving financial stability. By diversifying income sources, individuals can reduce financial risk, increase earning potential, and build a more robust financial foundation. This approach not only supports long-term wealth creation but also fosters a mindset of continuous improvement and innovation. As Ecclesiastes 11:2 wisely advises, investing in multiple ventures is a prudent way to protect oneself from the uncertainties of life, ensuring a secure and prosperous future.

The Law of Attraction is a principle that suggests that like attracts like, meaning that positive thoughts and beliefs can attract positive outcomes. While it is often associated with personal development, it is also relevant to wealth building. A prosperity mindset aligns with the Law of Attraction by fostering positive expectations and a belief in one's ability to achieve financial success. As motivational speaker Earl Nightingale once said, "We become what we think about." This quote highlights the importance of maintaining a positive, wealth-oriented mindset. By focusing on abundance, success, and opportunity, individuals can attract the resources, people, and circumstances needed to build wealth, a concept that echoes Proverbs 23:7, "For as he thinks in his heart, so is he."

The concept of mindset and its impact on financial independence is a powerful one, deeply rooted in both modern psychology and ancient wisdom. Our beliefs about money, wealth, and our own capabilities can significantly influence our financial outcomes. This idea is not new - it can be traced back to ancient texts, including the Hebrew Bible. In the book of Proverbs, we find numerous references to the power of mindset in relation to wealth and prosperity. Proverbs 23:7 states, "For as he thinks in his heart, so is he." This verse underscores the importance of our internal thoughts and beliefs in shaping our reality, including our financial reality. Similarly, Proverbs 4:23 advises, "Above all else, guard your heart, for everything you do flows from it." These verses suggest that our core beliefs and attitudes - our mindset - are fundamental to our actions and outcomes. Modern financial experts echo this ancient wisdom. T. Harv Eker, author of "Secrets of the Millionaire Mind," asserts, "Your income can grow only to the extent you do." This aligns with the biblical principle of personal growth and responsibility. The story of Joseph in Genesis provides a powerful example of how mindset can influence financial outcomes. Despite being sold into slavery and later imprisoned, Joseph maintained a mindset of diligence and wisdom. This ultimately led him to become the second most powerful man in Egypt, responsible for managing the nation's resources during a time of famine (Genesis 41:41-57).

The concept of abundance versus scarcity mindset is particularly relevant to financial independence. In Deuteronomy 8:18, we read, "But remember the Lord your God, for it is he who gives you the ability to produce wealth." This verse encourages an abundance mindset, recognizing that resources and opportunities for wealth creation are available. Contrast this with the scarcity mindset displayed by the Israelites in the desert, who despite being provided with manna, still hoarded it out of fear (Exodus 16:19-20). Carol Dweck, a Stanford psychologist known for her work on mindset, distinguishes between a fixed mindset and a growth mindset. Those with a growth mindset believe their abilities can be developed through dedication and hard work. This concept is mirrored in the biblical narrative of the talents (Matthew 25:14-30), where those who invested and grew their resources were rewarded, while the one who buried his talent out of fear was chastised. Financial independence often requires overcoming limiting beliefs and adopting a mindset of possibility. The story of Gideon in Judges 6-8 illustrates this transformation. Initially, Gideon saw himself as the least in his family, but with a shift in mindset and faith, he became a mighty warrior and leader. Similarly, many modern success stories, like that of Oprah Winfrey who rose from poverty to become one of the most influential media moguls, demonstrate the power of mindset in achieving financial independence. Developing a mindset conducive to financial independence also involves cultivating patience and long-term thinking. Proverbs 13:11 wisely notes, "Dishonest money dwindles away, but whoever gathers money little by little makes it grow." This aligns with the modern investment principle of compound interest, famously described by Albert Einstein as the "eighth wonder of the world."

The interplay between mindset and financial independence is a theme that transcends time, echoing from ancient biblical wisdom to modern psychological and financial insights. By cultivating a growth mindset, embracing abundance thinking, and aligning our beliefs with our financial goals, we can create a strong foundation for achieving and maintaining financial independence.

Chapter 3. Mindset Matters

Reflective Questions

1. How do my current beliefs about money and wealth influence my financial decisions?

Reflect on whether your beliefs are empowering or limiting your financial growth.

2. What specific financial goals have I set for myself, and how clear and actionable are they?

Consider whether your goals are SMART (Specific, Measurable, Achievable, Relevant, and Time-bound).

3. How do I respond to financial setbacks or challenges?

Assess your level of resilience and whether you view setbacks as opportunities to learn and grow.

4. Am I practicing delayed gratification in my financial life?

Reflect on how often you prioritize long-term goals over immediate desires.

5. In what ways am I cultivating gratitude for my current financial situation?

Consider how gratitude influences your financial decisions and overall mindset.

6. What steps am I taking to diversify my income streams?

Reflect on whether you are exploring multiple income opportunities to enhance financial security.

7. How do I invest in my personal and professional development to improve my financial well-being?

Consider how continuous learning and skill development contribute to your wealth-building efforts.

8. Do I regularly review and adjust my financial plans to align with changing circumstances?

Reflect on how adaptable and proactive you are in managing your finances.

9. How do I manage financial risks, and what is my approach to balancing risk and reward?

Consider your risk tolerance and whether you are taking calculated risks to grow your wealth.

10. How do I align my financial goals with my personal values and life purpose?

Reflect on whether your wealth-building efforts are in harmony with your broader life goals and principles.

Chapter 4:
Understanding Wealth Creation

Wealth creation is often perceived as the accumulation of financial assets, but a broader and more accurate understanding encompasses a wide range of factors that contribute to a well-rounded and fulfilling life. Wealth is not merely about having money; it's about achieving a balance of financial stability, health, personal fulfillment, and strong relationships. To truly grasp the concept of wealth creation, one must recognize the interconnectedness of these elements. Financial resources are crucial, but without good health, supportive relationships, and personal satisfaction, they can feel hollow. The journey to wealth creation involves cultivating these various aspects of life in harmony, ensuring that financial gains contribute to a greater sense of well-being and life satisfaction. This approach shifts the focus from simply accumulating assets to building a life rich in experiences, security, and happiness.

At the core of wealth creation lies the foundation of education and continuous learning. In a world that is constantly evolving, the ability to adapt and grow is vital for both personal and professional success. Education is not just about formal degrees; it encompasses the ongoing process of acquiring new knowledge, skills, and competencies. Whether through traditional academic routes, vocational training, or self-directed learning, investing in education pays dividends by enhancing your ability to navigate a complex and changing world. Continuous learning helps you stay relevant in your career, opens up new opportunities, and fosters innovation. It is through education that you build the tools needed to identify opportunities, solve problems, and create value in ways that contribute to long-term wealth. A commitment to lifelong learning keeps your mind agile and adaptable, qualities that are essential in a fast-paced global economy.

Education plays a significant role in wealth creation, often correlating with higher earning potential and increased opportunities. Recent data illustrates this relationship clearly. As of 2022, workers aged 25 and over without a high school diploma earned a median weekly income of $682. In contrast, those with a high school diploma earned $853 per week—a 25% increase over non-graduates. This trend continues with each level of education attained. While individual experiences may vary based on factors such as occupation or field of study, higher levels of education generally open doors to better-paying positions and career advancement opportunities. Beyond the direct impact on earnings, education provides valuable skills and knowledge that contribute to wealth creation. It enhances critical thinking, problem-solving abilities, and specialized expertise in chosen fields. These skills not only make individuals more valuable in the job market but also equip them to make informed financial decisions and identify wealth-building opportunities. Educational achievements serve as indicators to potential employers. They demonstrate an individual's ability to set long-term goals, meet deadlines, and complete complex tasks all qualities highly valued in the professional world.

This can lead to increased trust from employers, potentially resulting in more responsibilities and higher-paying positions. It's important to note that formal education isn't the only path to knowledge and skill acquisition. In today's digital age, numerous alternative learning opportunities exist, including online courses, workshops, and self-directed study. The key is to embrace lifelong learning, continuously updating your skills and knowledge to remain competitive and adaptable in an ever-changing economic landscape. While education alone doesn't guarantee wealth, it provides a strong foundation and numerous advantages on the path to financial success. By investing in your education and continuously expanding your knowledge base, you're investing in your potential for long-term wealth creation. Education has a profound impact on wealth creation, influencing an individual's earning potential, career opportunities, and financial stability over the course of a lifetime. Here's how education affects wealth:

Increased Earning Potential

One of the most direct ways education affects wealth is through increased earning potential. Studies consistently show that individuals with higher levels of education, such as bachelor's degrees, master's degrees, or professional certifications, tend to earn significantly more over their lifetimes than those with only a high school diploma or less. Education provides individuals with specialized knowledge and skills that are highly valued in the job market, making them more competitive for higher-paying positions. As a result, educated individuals often have greater income, which is a key factor in building and sustaining wealth.

Financial Stability and Security

Education contributes to financial stability by equipping individuals with the knowledge and skills to make informed financial decisions. Educated individuals are more likely to understand the importance of budgeting, saving, and investing, which are essential practices for building and maintaining wealth. Furthermore, education often leads to jobs with better benefits, such as health insurance, retirement plans, and job security, all of which contribute to long-term financial security. This stability reduces the risk of financial hardships and enables individuals to build wealth more effectively over time.

Entrepreneurial Opportunities

Education can also foster entrepreneurial opportunities, even though entrepreneurship itself isn't the focus here. Educated individuals often have the skills, knowledge, and networks needed to start and run successful businesses. Education provides the critical thinking, problem-solving, and leadership abilities necessary to innovate and take calculated risks. While not all educated individuals become entrepreneurs, those who do are often better prepared to succeed, potentially leading to significant wealth creation.

Intergenerational Wealth

The benefits of education extend beyond the individual, often leading to intergenerational wealth. Educated parents are more likely to emphasize the importance of education to their children, who then pursue higher levels of education themselves. This creates a cycle where each generation is better equipped to build wealth, leading to greater financial security and prosperity over time. Additionally, the wealth created by one generation through education can be passed down, further contributing to the economic stability and opportunities available to future generations.

Social and Economic Mobility

Education is a powerful tool for social and economic mobility, allowing individuals to improve their financial situation regardless of their starting point. By providing access to higher-paying jobs and the knowledge needed to manage finances effectively, education enables individuals to move up the economic ladder. This upward mobility is essential for breaking the cycle of poverty and achieving long-term wealth creation.

Adaptability in a Changing Economy

In today's rapidly changing economy, education is crucial for adaptability. As industries evolve and new technologies emerge, individuals with a strong educational foundation are better equipped to learn new skills and transition into different roles. This adaptability not only protects against job displacement but also opens up new opportunities for wealth creation in emerging sectors. Continuous education, whether formal or through lifelong learning, ensures that individuals remain relevant in the job market and can take advantage of new economic trends.

Education profoundly influences wealth by increasing earning potential, enabling career advancement, ensuring financial stability, fostering entrepreneurial opportunities, supporting intergenerational wealth, promoting social mobility, and enhancing adaptability. Investing in education is one of the most effective strategies for building and sustaining wealth over a lifetime.

A significant avenue for wealth creation is career advancement. Your career is not just a source of income; it is also a platform for personal growth, skill development, and the creation of a professional network. Climbing the career ladder can lead to increased financial rewards, but it also involves strategic planning, skill enhancement, and a proactive approach to opportunities. As Warren Buffett, one of the most successful investors of all time, once said, "The best investment you can make is in yourself." This sentiment underscores the importance of continuous personal and professional development in career advancement. In today's

competitive job market, advancing your career often requires continuous professional development, whether through acquiring new certifications, expanding your expertise, or taking on leadership roles. This aligns with the advice of former General Electric CEO Jack Welch, who stated, "An organization's ability to learn, and translate that learning into action rapidly, is the ultimate competitive advantage." Additionally, effective networking plays a critical role in career growth. Building and maintaining strong professional relationships can open doors to new opportunities, provide valuable insights, and support your career trajectory. As the saying goes, "Your network is your net worth." This phrase, often attributed to various business leaders, highlights the direct connection between professional relationships and wealth creation. Keith Ferrazzi, author of "Never Eat Alone," emphasizes this point: "The currency of real networking is not greed but generosity." This perspective encourages a mindset of mutual benefit and long-term relationship building in professional networks. By actively managing your career, seeking out challenges, and positioning yourself as a valuable asset to your organization or industry, you can significantly enhance your earning potential and overall wealth. This proactive approach is echoed in the words of Facebook COO Sheryl Sandberg: "If you're offered a seat on a rocket ship, don't ask what seat! Just get on." Career advancement also involves strategic risk-taking and stepping out of your comfort zone. Richard Branson, founder of the Virgin Group, advises, "If somebody offers you an amazing opportunity but you are not sure you can do it, say yes, then learn how to do it later!" This mindset encourages seizing opportunities for growth, even when they seem challenging. Moreover, career advancement often requires adaptability and a willingness to evolve with industry trends. As Alvin Toffler, futurist and author, famously said, "The illiterate of the 21st century will not be those who cannot read and write, but those who cannot learn, unlearn, and relearn." This highlights the importance of staying current and flexible in your career path. Leadership development is another crucial aspect of career advancement. John C. Maxwell, leadership expert, states, "The pessimist complains about the wind. The optimist expects it to change. The leader adjusts the sails." Developing leadership skills not only positions you for higher-level roles but also increases your value to employers. Finally, it's important to remember that career advancement is a journey, not a destination. As motivational speaker Zig Ziglar put it, "There is no elevator to success. You have to take the stairs." This reminds us that career growth and wealth creation through your profession often require patience, persistence, and consistent effort over time. By embracing these principles of career advancement, continuous learning, networking, seizing opportunities, developing leadership skills, and maintaining persistence, you can leverage your career as a powerful tool for wealth creation. Remember, your career is not just about earning a paycheck; it's about building a foundation for long-term financial success and personal fulfillment. Career advancement is a cornerstone of wealth creation, offering a path to increased earnings and personal development. Your career is more than just a job; it's an asset that, when managed strategically, can yield significant returns over time.

As Peter Drucker, the father of modern management, once said, "The best way to predict the future is to create it." This philosophy applies perfectly to career advancement. By taking proactive steps to shape your professional trajectory, you're effectively creating your future wealth. One crucial aspect of career advancement is the development of a growth mindset. Carol Dweck, psychologist and author, explains, "In a growth mindset, challenges are exciting rather than threatening. So rather than thinking, oh, I'm going to reveal my weaknesses, you say, wow, here's a chance to grow." This attitude can help you embrace new challenges and learn from setbacks, both of which are inevitable in any career journey. Skill diversification is another key component of career advancement. T-shaped professionals, who have deep expertise in one area and broad knowledge in many others, are increasingly valued in today's job market. As Steve Jobs famously said, "Technology alone is not enough. Its technology married with the liberal arts, married with the humanities, that yields the results that make our hearts sing." This interdisciplinary approach can make you a more versatile and valuable employee. In the digital age, technological literacy has become crucial across almost all industries. Eric Schmidt, former CEO of Google, emphasizes this point: "The race is on to become a digital native, and if you don't do it, I'm going to guarantee your company won't be here in a meaningful way in ten years." Staying ahead of technological trends can give you a significant advantage in your career progression. "While mastering technical skills and gaining experience are crucial for career advancement, cultivating Emotional Intelligence is equally essential, as it enables you to navigate complex workplace dynamics, build stronger relationships, and lead with empathy, ultimately driving sustained success in your career."

Emotional intelligence (EQ) has become a cornerstone of career success, especially in leadership roles and navigating complex workplace dynamics. Unlike traditional measures of intelligence, such as IQ, which focus on cognitive abilities like problem-solving and analytical thinking, EQ encompasses the ability to understand and manage your own emotions as well as those of others. This holistic approach to emotional and social functioning is increasingly valued in the workplace, where collaboration, communication, and interpersonal relationships are essential for success. Daniel Goleman, who popularized the concept of emotional intelligence, identifies five key components: self-awareness, self-regulation, motivation, empathy, and social skills. Each of these elements plays a crucial role in how individuals interact with others and handle challenges in their professional lives.

1. Self-Awareness: This is the ability to recognize and understand your own emotions, strengths, weaknesses, and values. Self-aware individuals are better equipped to manage their emotions in challenging situations, which can prevent conflicts and promote a more positive work environment. For example, a self-aware leader can recognize when they are feeling stressed and take steps to manage it without letting it affect their decision-making or interactions with their team.

2. Self-Regulation: Self-regulation involves managing your emotions and impulses in a healthy way. It's about being in control of your emotional responses, even in high-pressure situations. This ability is crucial in maintaining professionalism and composure, particularly when dealing with difficult situations or people. Leaders who can self-regulate are more likely to earn the trust and respect of their colleagues, as they are seen as stable and reliable.

3. Motivation: Individuals with high EQ are often driven by internal motivation rather than external rewards. They have a passion for their work, a strong drive to achieve, and a commitment to their goals. This intrinsic motivation can be a powerful force in pushing through challenges and maintaining focus, even when faced with setbacks.

4. Empathy: Empathy is the ability to understand and share the feelings of others. It allows individuals to connect with their colleagues on a deeper level, fostering strong relationships and collaboration. In the workplace, empathy is essential for effective communication, conflict resolution, and team cohesion. Leaders with high empathy can better understand the needs and concerns of their team members, which enables them to provide the appropriate support and guidance.

5. Social Skills: Social skills encompass a range of abilities, including communication, conflict management, teamwork, and the ability to build and maintain relationships. People with strong social skills can effectively navigate social complexities in the workplace, influence others positively, and lead by example. These skills are particularly important for leaders, as they must be able to inspire and motivate their teams, build consensus, and drive collective success.

Emotional intelligence can significantly enhance career success by improving relationships, fostering collaboration, and enhancing leadership capabilities. In today's work environment, technical skills alone are often not enough to excel. Employers increasingly value employees who can work well with others, handle stress effectively, and adapt to changing circumstances, all of which are facilitated by high EQ.

- Enhanced Leadership Potential: Leaders with high EQ are more effective because they can manage their own emotions while also understanding and influencing the emotions of others. This ability is crucial for building trust, inspiring teams, and driving organizational success. Leaders with high EQ are often better at conflict resolution, making them more capable of leading diverse teams and managing change within an organization.
- Improved Workplace Dynamics: In any workplace, relationships and communication are key to success. High EQ individuals are skilled at reading social cues, understanding group dynamics, and responding to the needs of their colleagues. This makes them invaluable in roles that require teamwork and collaboration. By fostering a positive and supportive work environment, individuals with high EQ contribute to higher employee morale, greater job satisfaction, and improved productivity.
- Better Decision-Making: Emotional intelligence also plays a role in decision-making. By being aware of their emotions and the emotions of others, individuals with high EQ can

make more informed and balanced decisions. They are less likely to be swayed by emotional impulses and more capable of considering the long-term impact of their choices. This leads to better outcomes for both the individual and the organization.

Developing Emotional Intelligence

While some aspects of emotional intelligence may be innate, it is also a skill that can be developed and enhanced over time. This involves self-reflection, mindfulness, and a commitment to personal growth. Some strategies for developing EQ include:

- Practicing mindfulness to become more aware of your emotions and how they influence your thoughts and behavior.
- Seeking feedback from others to gain a better understanding of how your emotional responses affect your interactions and relationships.
- Improving communication skills to express your thoughts and feelings more clearly and listen more effectively to others.
- Developing empathy by actively trying to see things from others' perspectives and considering their feelings and needs in your decision-making.

By prioritizing the development of emotional intelligence, you can enhance your career prospects, improve your leadership abilities, and create more meaningful and effective relationships in the workplace. As Daniel Goleman's work suggests, those who master their emotions and cultivate strong interpersonal skills are better positioned to succeed, regardless of their cognitive intelligence.

The freelance market and remote work have opened up new avenues for career advancement and wealth creation. As Seth Godin, entrepreneur and author, puts it, "The job is what you do when you are told what to do. The job is showing up at the factory, following instructions, meeting spec, and being managed.

Someone can always do your job a little better or faster or cheaper than you can. The job might be difficult, it might require skill, but it's a job. Your art is what you do when no one can tell you exactly how to do it. Your art is the act of taking personal responsibility, challenging the status quo, and changing people." This perspective encourages thinking beyond traditional employment structures and considering entrepreneurial paths. Continuous learning is crucial for sustained career growth. In the words of Satya Nadella, CEO of Microsoft, "The learn-it-all does better than the know-it-all." This mindset of perpetual learning can help you stay relevant and adaptable in a rapidly changing job

market. Building a personal brand can significantly boost your career prospects. As Jeff Bezos, founder of Amazon, says, "Your brand is what people say about you when you're not in the room." Cultivating a strong professional reputation can open doors to new opportunities and increase your perceived value in the job market. Finally, it's important to align your career choices with your personal values and long-term goals. As Oprah Winfrey advises, "You become what you believe. You are where you are today in your life based on everything you have believed." This alignment can lead to greater job satisfaction and motivation, which in turn can fuel your career advancement and wealth creation efforts. By embracing these multifaceted aspects of career development, from cultivating a growth mindset and diverse skill set to building your personal brand and aligning with your values, you can transform your career into a powerful engine for wealth creation. Remember, in the words of Malcolm Gladwell, "Practice isn't the thing you do once you're good. It's the thing you do that makes you good." Consistent effort and strategic planning in your career can lead to substantial rewards over time. In the pursuit of wealth creation, your skills and expertise are among your most valuable assets. Developing and honing these abilities allows you to create value in the marketplace, whether through your job, a side project, or other endeavors. The key to leveraging your skills lies in understanding your strengths and identifying how they can be applied in ways that meet market demand. This could involve specializing in a niche area where your skills are highly valued or broadening your expertise to increase your versatility. As you advance in your career, it's important to continue refining your skills and staying updated with industry trends. This not only makes you more competitive in the job market but also positions you to take advantage of new opportunities as they arise. By aligning your skills with market needs, you can enhance your earning potential and contribute to your long-term wealth creation goals.

A strong professional network is one of the most valuable assets in wealth creation, offering far more than just a list of contacts. It opens doors to opportunities, resources, and support that can profoundly influence your career trajectory and financial success. Networking transcends the mere exchange of business cards or LinkedIn connections; it's about nurturing meaningful relationships that foster collaboration, mentorship, and career advancement. These relationships become the backbone of your professional life, providing the insights and guidance needed to navigate the complexities of your industry. A well-developed network is like having a personal advisory board at your fingertips. It grants you access to insider knowledge, such as emerging industry trends, job openings, and potential partnerships that might not be publicly advertised. This information can give you a competitive edge, allowing you to act on opportunities before others even know they exist. Whether you're looking to switch careers, start a new business, or scale an existing venture, the connections within your network can be instrumental in accelerating these processes. They can introduce you to key stakeholders, provide critical feedback, or even serve as partners or investors in your endeavors. However, effective networking is a two-way street. It's not just about what you can gain, but also about what you can offer. Providing value to your network, whether through sharing your expertise,

making introductions, or offering support, creates a foundation of trust and mutual benefit. This reciprocal relationship ensures that your network remains active and engaged, rather than becoming stagnant. By consistently giving value, you build a reputation as a reliable and valuable contact, making others more likely to support you when you need it. The strength of your network can also be a critical factor in navigating career transitions or exploring new business opportunities. When you face challenges, whether it's a job loss, a difficult project, or the need to pivot your business, your network can offer the guidance, resources, and encouragement needed to overcome these obstacles. The support from a trusted network can make the difference between struggling alone and having a team of allies who are invested in your success. A robust professional network is an essential component of wealth creation, providing access to opportunities and support that can significantly enhance your career and financial outcomes. By cultivating relationships built on trust, mutual benefit, and the consistent exchange of value, you create a powerful network of allies who are committed to helping you achieve your goals. This network becomes a critical resource, enabling you to navigate the ever-changing landscape of your professional life with confidence and resilience.

Understanding the value of time is a fundamental aspect of wealth creation. Time is a finite resource, and how you choose to spend it can significantly impact your financial success. The concept of time value is rooted in the idea that the earlier you start working towards your financial goals, the greater the potential for wealth accumulation over time. This principle is particularly evident in the power of compound interest, where even small investments made early can grow exponentially if given enough time. By recognizing that time is one of your most valuable assets, you can make more informed decisions about how to allocate it, whether through investing, acquiring new skills, or pursuing opportunities that align with your long-term financial goals. Additionally, the value of time in wealth creation extends beyond just financial investments. It also involves how you manage your time in everyday life. Prioritizing tasks that contribute to your financial well-being, such as budgeting, planning, and continuous learning, can lead to more efficient wealth-building strategies.

Conversely, spending time on activities that do not align with your financial objectives can delay or diminish your wealth creation efforts. Time management, therefore, becomes a critical skill in maximizing your financial potential. Understanding the value of time encourages a long-term perspective on wealth creation. It shifts the focus from immediate gratification to future financial security, emphasizing the importance of patience, persistence, and discipline. Building wealth is often a gradual process that requires consistent effort over time. Those who appreciate the value of time are more likely to stay committed to their financial plans, even when progress seems slow. They understand that wealth is not typically built overnight, but rather through steady, intentional actions taken over many years. In the context of career development, the value of time also manifests in the strategic choices you make regarding your professional growth. Investing time in education, skill development, and building a professional network can pay dividends in the form of higher earning potential and greater opportunities for advancement. Each career decision should be viewed through the lens of its long-term impact on your financial well-being, recognizing that the time you invest now can yield significant returns in the future. Ultimately, understanding the value of time in wealth creation is about recognizing that every moment is an opportunity to move closer to your financial goals. Whether through investing, improving your skills, or making strategic life choices, how you use your time today will shape your financial future. By valuing time as a critical component of wealth creation, you can make decisions that maximize your financial potential and ensure long-term prosperity.

In the journey to wealth creation, adaptability and resilience are critical qualities that enable you to navigate the inevitable challenges and changes that arise. The ability to adapt to new circumstances, whether technological advancements, economic shifts, or personal life changes, ensures that you remain relevant and capable of seizing new opportunities. Resilience, on the other hand, is the capacity to recover from setbacks and continue pursuing your goals despite obstacles. Together, these traits help you maintain a forward momentum, even in the face of adversity. Developing adaptability might involve learning new skills, exploring different career paths, or rethinking your approach to challenges. Building resilience requires a mindset that views failures as learning experiences and maintains focus on long-term objectives. By cultivating adaptability and resilience, you enhance your ability to sustain and grow your wealth over time, regardless of external circumstances. In the journey to wealth creation, adaptability and resilience are vital qualities that empower you to navigate the inevitable challenges and changes that arise. Life is full of unexpected twists, and the ability to adapt to new circumstances, whether they be technological advancements, economic shifts, or personal life changes, ensures that you remain relevant and capable of seizing new opportunities. As John F. Kennedy wisely observed, "Change is the law of life. And those who look only to the past or present are certain to miss the future." This insight underscores the importance of adaptability, which might involve learning new skills, exploring different career paths, or rethinking your approach to challenges in order to stay ahead of the curve. Resilience, on the other hand, is equally essential, as it embodies the capacity to recover from setbacks and persist in the pursuit of your financial goals. As the motivational speaker Zig Ziglar once said, "Failure is a detour, not a dead-end street." This perspective is crucial in wealth creation, where obstacles and failures are a natural part of the journey. Building resilience requires cultivating a mindset that views failures not as final verdicts, but as valuable learning experiences that can inform your future decisions and strategies. By maintaining focus on long-term objectives and refusing to be deterred by short-term setbacks, you develop the perseverance necessary to overcome challenges and achieve sustained success. Together, adaptability and resilience create a powerful synergy that allows you to maintain forward momentum, even in the face of adversity. Developing these traits involves a continuous commitment to personal growth and a willingness to embrace change. Adaptability might require staying informed about industry trends, updating your skillset to meet new demands, or being open to opportunities that align with your financial aspirations. Meanwhile, resilience demands a mindset of optimism and

determination, recognizing that setbacks are part of the process and can ultimately make you stronger. By cultivating adaptability and resilience, you enhance your ability to sustain and grow your wealth over time, regardless of external circumstances. These qualities not only enable you to withstand the pressures and uncertainties of the wealth creation journey but also empower you to thrive by turning challenges into opportunities. As Helen Keller famously said, "Although the world is full of suffering, it is also full of the overcoming of it." Embracing adaptability and resilience equips you with the tools to not just survive but to succeed and flourish, even when faced with the most daunting challenges. Resilience is the steadfast ability to bounce back from setbacks and persevere in the face of adversity, ultimately transforming obstacles into opportunities and paving the way for enduring success.

Discipline and patience are two virtues that play a pivotal role in the wealth creation process. Discipline involves making consistent, intentional choices that align with your long-term goals, whether it's saving money, investing in education, or managing your time effectively. As Jim Rohn famously said, "Discipline is the bridge between goals and accomplishment." This quote encapsulates the essence of discipline: it requires adhering to a plan, even when it is challenging, and resisting the allure of short-term gratification that can derail your progress. The commitment to disciplined actions, whether in budgeting, investing, or skill development, lays the foundation for sustained success.

Patience, on the other hand, is the virtue that complements discipline by allowing your efforts the time to bear fruit. As Warren Buffett aptly noted, "The stock market is designed to transfer money from the Active to the Patient." This observation highlights that the wealth creation journey is often gradual and requires waiting for your disciplined actions to yield results. The compounding effects of your efforts, whether they involve career growth, skill acquisition, or financial investments, take time to manifest fully. Patience helps you remain steadfast and optimistic as you navigate the long-term process of wealth building. Together, discipline and patience form a powerful combination that ensures you stay on course and build sustainable wealth. Discipline provides the framework and consistency needed to achieve your goals, while patience allows you to endure and appreciate the gradual accumulation of your efforts. By embodying these virtues, you enhance your ability to realize both your financial and personal aspirations, ultimately leading to enduring success. As the famous proverb goes, "Patience is not simply the ability to wait, it's how we behave while we're waiting." Embracing both discipline and patience equips you with the resilience to face challenges and the foresight to achieve long-term prosperity. "Patience and discipline are key pillars in both maintaining good health and building wealth, as cultivating healthy habits and making thoughtful financial decisions require consistent effort and a long-term perspective."

Your health and well-being are foundational to your ability to create and enjoy wealth. Physical health, mental clarity, and emotional balance are essential components that support your productivity, decision-making, and overall quality of life. As the ancient Roman poet Virgil

wisely stated, "The greatest wealth is health." Physical health is a cornerstone of wealth creation. Without it, even the most successful wealth-building efforts can be undermined, as poor health can lead to increased medical costs, reduced ability to work, and diminished life satisfaction. Jim Rohn, entrepreneur and motivational speaker, emphasized this point: "Take care of your body. It's the only place you have to live." Maintaining a healthy lifestyle through regular exercise, a balanced diet, and adequate rest is not only beneficial for your well-being but also enhances your ability to perform at your best in both your personal and professional life. As Richard Branson, founder of Virgin Group, advises, "If you want to be more productive, you need to take care of your body, and you need to take care of your mind. "The importance of sleep-in maintaining health and productivity cannot be overstated. Arianna Huffington, co-founder of The Huffington Post, learned this lesson the hard way and now advocates strongly for proper rest: "Sleep is a fundamental and non-negotiable human need. The decimation of sleep throughout industrialized nations is having a catastrophic impact on our health, our job performance, our relationships, and our happiness." Mental health is equally crucial in the wealth creation journey. Managing stress, cultivating a positive mindset, and seeking support when needed are vital for sustaining long-term productivity and success. As the Dalai Lama wisely noted, "If you have peace of mind, when you meet with problems and difficulties, they won't disturb your inner peace. You'll be able to employ your human intelligence more effectively." Stress management is a key aspect of maintaining mental health. Hans Selye, a pioneering endocrinologist, observed, "It's not stress that kills us, it is our reaction to it." Learning effective stress management techniques can significantly improve your resilience and performance in high-pressure situations often encountered in wealth-building endeavors.

Emotional intelligence plays a crucial role in both health and wealth creation. Daniel Goleman, psychologist and author, explains, "If your emotional abilities aren't in hand, if you don't have self-awareness, if you are not able to manage your distressing emotions, if you can't have empathy and have effective relationships, then no matter how smart you are, you are not going to get very far. "The mind-body connection is increasingly recognized as a critical factor in overall health and performance. As Jon Kabat-Zinn, professor and mindfulness expert, states, "You can't stop the waves, but you can learn to surf." This metaphor aptly describes the importance of developing mental resilience and adaptability in the face of life's challenges, including those encountered on the path to wealth creation. Nutrition also plays a vital role in maintaining health and cognitive function. As Ann Wigmore, holistic health practitioner, said, "The food you eat can be either the safest and most powerful form of medicine or the slowest form of poison." Making informed dietary choices can significantly impact your energy levels, mental clarity, and long-term health outcomes. Regular physical activity is not just beneficial for physical health but also for cognitive function and emotional well-being. John J. Ratey, associate clinical professor of psychiatry at Harvard Medical School, explains, "Exercise is the single most powerful tool you have to optimize your brain function." Incorporating regular exercise into your routine can enhance your problem-solving abilities, creativity, and overall productivity.

Work-life balance is another crucial aspect of maintaining health while pursuing wealth. As Anne-Marie Slaughter, foreign policy expert and work-life balance advocate, points out, "I think we need to rethink our entire concept of balance. 'Balance' suggests a perfect equilibrium. For many of us, that is impossible to achieve given the demands on our time and energy." By prioritizing your health and well-being, you ensure that you have the energy, focus, and resilience needed to pursue your wealth creation goals effectively. Remember the words of Warren Buffett: "When you get to my age, you'll really measure your success in life by how many of the people you want to have love you actually do love you. That's the ultimate test of how you have lived your life. "Health and wealth are inextricably linked. As you embark on your wealth creation journey, consider the words of Mahatma Gandhi: "It is health that is real wealth and not pieces of gold and silver." By investing in your physical, mental, and emotional well-being, you're laying a solid foundation for sustainable wealth creation and a truly prosperous life.

Understanding wealth creation involves recognizing and harnessing a range of fundamental principles and qualities that contribute to long-term financial success. At its core, wealth creation is not just about accumulating money but about building a sustainable and fulfilling financial future. The journey begins with a clear understanding of the value of time, acknowledging that early and consistent efforts can lead to exponential growth through mechanisms like compound interest. Effective wealth creation also hinges on continuous learning and adaptability, as the ability to embrace new technologies, economic shifts, and evolving personal circumstances ensures relevance and opportunity in a constantly changing landscape. Equally important are the qualities of discipline and patience. Discipline drives consistent, intentional actions aligned with long-term goals, enabling you to make wise financial decisions and avoid the pitfalls of short-term gratification. As Jim Rohn aptly put it, "Discipline is the bridge between goals and accomplishment." Patience complements this by allowing you to wait for your disciplined efforts to yield significant returns, acknowledging that wealth creation is often a gradual process. Warren Buffett's observation that "The stock market is designed to transfer money from the Active to the Patient" underscores the importance of enduring persistence in achieving financial success. Resilience and adaptability are crucial traits that further bolster your wealth creation journey. Resilience enables you to recover from setbacks and persevere in the face of obstacles, transforming challenges into opportunities for growth. As Zig Ziglar noted, "Failure is a detour, not a dead-end street," emphasizing that setbacks are not final but integral to the learning process. Adaptability ensures that you can navigate changes and seize new opportunities, embodying the principle that "Change is the law of life," as stated by John F. Kennedy. Together, these qualities ensure that you remain agile and prepared, no matter what circumstances arise. Finally, a strong professional network plays a vital role in wealth creation by providing access to valuable opportunities, resources, and support. The essence of effective networking is to build meaningful relationships that foster collaboration, mentorship, and career advancement. As Helen Keller insightfully observed, "Although the

world is full of suffering, it is also full of the overcoming of it," highlighting the power of resilience and support from your network in overcoming challenges. In conclusion, understanding wealth creation is a multifaceted endeavor that integrates time management, continuous learning, discipline, patience, adaptability, and networking. By cultivating these attributes and embracing the principles they represent, you can build a robust foundation for financial success and personal fulfillment. Wealth creation is a journey that requires persistence, strategic planning, and the ability to adapt and grow, ultimately leading to a prosperous and rewarding financial future.

Chapter 4. Understanding Wealth Creation

Reflective Questions

1. How do I currently manage my time in relation to my financial goals, and what changes can I make to better leverage the value of time in my wealth creation strategy?

2. In what ways have I demonstrated adaptability in my personal or professional life, and how can I apply these experiences to enhance my approach to wealth creation?

3. What are some recent challenges or setbacks I have faced, and how have my resilience and mindset contributed to my ability to overcome these obstacles?

4. How do I balance short-term gratification with long-term financial goals, and what strategies can I implement to strengthen my discipline in wealth creation?

5. What role does patience play in my financial planning, and how can I cultivate a mindset that supports long-term perseverance and delayed gratification?

6. How effectively am I utilizing my professional network to support my wealth creation goals, and what steps can I take to strengthen and expand these connections?

7. What skills or knowledge gaps do I have that might be hindering my progress in wealth creation, and how can I address these gaps through further education or training?

8. How do I respond to changes in my environment, such as technological advancements or economic shifts, and what strategies can I develop to stay ahead in a dynamic landscape?

9. In what ways have my disciplined actions contributed to my financial success so far, and how can I enhance my commitment to these actions to achieve my long-term objectives?

10. Reflecting on past failures or setbacks, what valuable lessons have I learned, and how can these insights inform my future approach to overcoming challenges and achieving wealth creation goals?

Chapter 5:
Embracing Entrepreneurship as a Path to Prosperity

Entrepreneurship is more than just the act of starting a business; it represents a transformative journey of innovation, resilience, and the relentless pursuit of one's passions. By turning ideas into tangible solutions, entrepreneurs not only create wealth for themselves but also contribute to the economy and society at large. The pursuit of entrepreneurship offers a powerful avenue for achieving financial independence and prosperity, allowing individuals to take control of their destinies and build something of lasting value. As Natalie Clifford Barney once said, "Entrepreneurship is the last refuge of the troublemaking individual," highlighting the boldness required to forge a new path. At the heart of entrepreneurship is a unique mindset characterized by creativity, risk-taking, and a commitment to continuous learning. Entrepreneurs see the world differently, viewing challenges as opportunities to innovate and grow. This mindset is essential for navigating the inevitable ups and downs of the entrepreneurial journey. Consider the example of Elon Musk, whose relentless pursuit of innovation led to the creation of multiple successful companies, from PayPal to Tesla and SpaceX. His willingness to take risks and think outside the box has revolutionized entire industries, embodying the entrepreneurial spirit. Albert Schweitzer captured this essence when he said, "Success is not the key to happiness. Happiness is the key to success. If you love what you are doing, you will be successful."

The path to prosperity through entrepreneurship is rarely smooth, and challenges are an inherent part of the journey. Financial constraints, market competition, and personal sacrifices are just a few of the hurdles that entrepreneurs must overcome. Building resilience is crucial for weathering these storms and staying the course. Sara Blakely, the founder of Spanx, exemplifies this resilience. After facing numerous rejections, her shapewear products finally gained traction, turning Spanx into a billion-dollar company. Her story illustrates the importance of persistence in the face of adversity. Henry Ford's words, "Failure is simply the opportunity to begin again, this time more intelligently," resonate deeply with the entrepreneurial experience. Here are some examples:

1. Financial Struggles:

Many entrepreneurs face financial difficulties, especially in the early stages of their businesses. For instance, James Dyson went through 5,126 failed prototypes and nearly bankrupted himself before finally creating his successful vacuum cleaner. He persevered through immense financial strain, demonstrating that even groundbreaking ideas often require substantial investment and risk.

2. Market Rejection:

Rejection from the market is a common challenge. Airbnb founders Brian Chesky and Joe Gebbia were initially dismissed by investors who couldn't envision people wanting to stay in

strangers' homes. They had to overcome skepticism and slowly build trust in their platform before achieving success.

3. Regulatory Hurdles:

Entrepreneurs often face complex regulatory environments. Uber, for example, has battled regulatory challenges in numerous cities worldwide. While controversial, their story illustrates how disruptive business models can face significant legal and regulatory obstacles.

4. Personal Sacrifice:

The demands of entrepreneurship often lead to personal sacrifices. Jeff Bezos left a lucrative job on Wall Street to start Amazon, working long hours and taking significant personal financial risks. His wife at the time, Mackenzie Scott, supported the family financially in the early years of Amazon's development.

5. Pivoting and Adaptation:

Many successful businesses look very different from their original concepts. Instagram, for instance, started as a location-based check-in app called Burbn before pivoting to focus solely on photo-sharing. This demonstrates how entrepreneurs must be willing to adapt their ideas based on market feedback.

6. Technological Challenges:

In the tech world, unforeseen technical issues can derail progress. Zappos founder Nick Swinmurn faced numerous technical difficulties in the early days of e-commerce, including website crashes during peak times. Overcoming these hurdles required persistence and creative problem-solving.

7. Economic Downturns:

External economic factors can pose significant challenges. Airbnb, for example, was founded just before the 2008 financial crisis. The founders had to be creative, even selling election-themed cereal to raise funds during this difficult period.

8. Scaling Challenges:

As businesses grow, entrepreneurs face new challenges in scaling operations. Howard Schultz, when expanding Starbucks, had to navigate the complexities of maintaining quality and culture while rapidly growing the business.

9. Work-Life Balance:

Many entrepreneurs struggle with work-life balance. Arianna Huffington, founder of The Huffington Post, famously collapsed from exhaustion, leading her to reevaluate her priorities and eventually start a new venture focused on well-being.

10. Self-Doubt:

Psychological challenges, including self-doubt, are common among entrepreneurs. Even successful entrepreneurs like Richard Branson have spoken about battling imposter syndrome and self-doubt throughout their careers.

As Reid Hoffman, co-founder of LinkedIn, aptly put it: "An entrepreneur is someone who jumps off a cliff and builds a plane on the way down." This quote captures the inherent risks and challenges of entrepreneurship, as well as the creativity and resilience required to succeed. These examples illustrate that the path to entrepreneurial success is indeed rarely smooth. However, they also demonstrate that with persistence, adaptability, and resilience, entrepreneurs can overcome significant obstacles to achieve their goals. The ability to learn from failures, pivot when necessary, and maintain focus on long-term vision are key attributes that help entrepreneurs navigate these challenges and ultimately find their path to prosperity.

Innovation is the lifeblood of entrepreneurship, driving growth and opening new avenues for wealth creation. Successful entrepreneurs constantly seek out new ways to solve problems, improve existing products or services, and meet the evolving needs of their customers. The role of innovation in entrepreneurship cannot be overstated, as it is often the key to staying competitive in a dynamic market. Apple Inc. serves as a prime example of innovation at its best. Steve Jobs and his team revolutionized technology with the introduction of the iPhone, transforming the way people communicate and access information. Jobs once remarked, "Innovation distinguishes between a leader and a follower," emphasizing the critical role of creative thinking in entrepreneurship. It's important to note that innovation in entrepreneurship extends far beyond just product development. It encompasses innovative business models, marketing strategies, and operational processes that can disrupt entire industries. For instance, Netflix's shift from DVD rentals to streaming services not only transformed the company but also revolutionized how people consume entertainment. This kind of innovation often requires a willingness to dismantle one's own successful products or services in pursuit of future growth. innovation in entrepreneurship is often sparked by identifying unmet needs or inefficiencies in existing systems. Uber, for example, recognized the inefficiencies in the traditional taxi industry and leveraged smartphone technology to create a more convenient and user-friendly transportation solution. This demonstrates how entrepreneurs can create value by reimagining established industries through the lens of emerging technologies.

The concept of "disruptive innovation," coined by Clayton Christensen, is particularly relevant in this context. It refers to innovations that create new markets and value networks, eventually disrupting existing ones. Airbnb's disruption of the hospitality industry is a prime example, showing how a novel approach to an existing service can reshape an entire sector. However, it's crucial to understand that innovation doesn't always mean inventing something entirely new. Often, it involves combining existing technologies or ideas in novel ways. Amazon's success, for instance, wasn't based on inventing e-commerce, but on innovating the online shopping experience through features like one-click purchasing and personalized recommendations. The importance of fostering a culture of innovation within an organization cannot be overstated. Companies like Google have become renowned for their innovative practices, such as allowing employees to spend 20% of their time on personal projects. This approach has led to the development of successful products like Gmail and Google News, illustrating how nurturing creativity across all levels of an organization can drive innovation. In the digital age, data-driven innovation has become increasingly important. Entrepreneurs are leveraging big data and analytics to gain insights into consumer behavior, optimize operations, and create personalized experiences. Companies like Amazon and Netflix use sophisticated algorithms to predict customer preferences and tailor their offerings accordingly, demonstrating how data can be a powerful tool for innovation. It's also worth noting that innovation in entrepreneurship isn't limited to the tech sector. In fields like sustainability and social entrepreneurship, innovators are finding creative solutions to pressing global challenges. For example, companies like Impossible Foods are innovating in food technology to create plant-based alternatives to meat, addressing both environmental concerns and changing consumer preferences. Lastly, the iterative nature of innovation in entrepreneurship is crucial to understand. The concept of "failing fast" and learning from mistakes is integral to the innovation process. As Reid Hoffman, co-founder of LinkedIn, famously said, "If you're not embarrassed by the first version of your product, you've launched too late." This mindset encourages entrepreneurs to release early versions of their products or services, gather feedback, and continuously iterate and improve.

Innovation is indeed the driving force behind successful entrepreneurship. It enables businesses to stay relevant, meet evolving customer needs, and create new value in the marketplace. Whether through groundbreaking technologies, novel business models, or creative problem-solving, innovation empowers entrepreneurs to turn their visions into reality and potentially reshape entire industries in the process. Bridging innovation with financial acumen, networking, and mentoring creates a powerful synergy that can propel entrepreneurs towards success. Innovative ideas, while crucial, require sound financial management to become viable businesses. Simultaneously, strong networks and mentorship can provide the support, guidance, and resources needed to bring these innovations to market effectively.

Consider the case of Airbnb founders Brian Chesky, Joe Gebbia, and Nathan Blecharczyk. Their innovative concept of turning spare rooms into short-term rentals disrupted the hospitality industry. However, it was their financial acumen that allowed them to navigate the challenging early days, including their creative "Obama O's" cereal fundraising campaign during the

2008 financial crisis. Furthermore, their ability to network and secure mentorship from Y Combinator's Paul Graham proved instrumental in refining their business model and securing crucial early-stage funding. This interplay is further exemplified by Spanx founder Sara Blakely. Her innovative product addressed an unmet need in the market, but it was her prudent financial management - starting the company with just $5,000 of her savings - that allowed her to maintain control and profitability from the outset. Blakely also credits much of her success to the mentorship she received from Richard Branson and other experienced entrepreneurs in her network. As Reid Hoffman, co-founder of LinkedIn, aptly puts it: "The fastest way to change yourself is to hang out with people who are already the way you want to be." This quote underscores how networking and mentorship can accelerate the learning curve for entrepreneurs, helping them to innovate more effectively and manage their finances more astutely. Financial acumen can itself drive innovation. Understanding financial constraints and opportunities can lead to creative solutions and new business models. For instance, the "freemium" model popularized by companies like Spotify and Dropbox is an innovative approach to monetization that requires a deep understanding of user acquisition costs, conversion rates, and lifetime customer value. In essence, successful entrepreneurship is about creating a cycle where innovation drives financial success, which in turn fuels further innovation. Networks and mentors provide the support structure and knowledge base to amplify this cycle. As Steve Jobs once said, "Innovation distinguishes between a leader and a follower," but it's the combination of innovation with financial savvy and strong relationships that truly sets successful entrepreneurs apart.

For entrepreneurs, effective financial management is a cornerstone of turning business success into lasting wealth. This involves not only generating revenue but also managing expenses, reinvesting profits, and planning for the future. Making wise financial decisions is essential for ensuring long-term prosperity and sustainability. Warren Buffett, known for his disciplined approach to investing and financial management, exemplifies this principle. His ability to identify profitable opportunities and manage his wealth prudently has made him one of the wealthiest individuals in the world. Buffett's advice, "Do not save what is left after spending, but spend what is left after saving," underscores the importance of financial discipline in entrepreneurship. In addition to financial acumen, building and leveraging strong networks is vital for entrepreneurial success. Mentorship, in particular, provides valuable guidance, support, and insight that can accelerate an entrepreneur's journey to prosperity. Networking opens doors to new opportunities, partnerships, and resources that might otherwise be inaccessible. Oprah Winfrey's career is a testament to the power of mentorship and networking. Her success was partly due to the mentors and networks she built throughout her career, which provided

her with opportunities and insights that helped her build a media empire. Oprah's philosophy, "Surround yourself with only people who are going to lift you higher," speaks to the importance of cultivating a supportive network. Building on this content, it's clear that financial acumen is a cornerstone of entrepreneurial success. Warren Buffett's approach to financial management goes beyond mere frugality; it encompasses a deep understanding of value investing and strategic capital allocation. Entrepreneurs can learn from Buffett's patient, long-term perspective on wealth creation. His famous quote, "Someone's sitting in the shade today because someone planted a tree a long time ago," emphasizes the importance of making wise financial decisions early on that will yield benefits in the future.

Financial acumen for entrepreneurs extends to various aspects of business management. It involves understanding cash flow management, which is often cited as one of the primary reasons small businesses fail. Effective entrepreneurs must be adept at forecasting cash needs, managing accounts receivable and payable, and maintaining adequate reserves to weather unexpected challenges. This skill becomes even more critical during periods of rapid growth, when cash flow can be strained despite increasing revenues. Financial literacy enables entrepreneurs to make informed decisions about funding their ventures. Whether it's bootstrapping, seeking venture capital, or taking on debt, each financing option comes with its own set of implications. Understanding these nuances allows entrepreneurs to choose the most appropriate funding strategy for their business at different stages of growth. For instance, Mark Zuckerberg's decision to maintain control of Facebook (now Meta) by limiting outside investment in the early days proved to be a crucial factor in the company's long-term success and his personal wealth accumulation. Financial acumen also plays a vital role in valuation and exit strategies. Entrepreneurs must be able to accurately assess the value of their businesses, whether for the purpose of raising capital, considering merger and acquisition opportunities, or planning an initial public offering (IPO). Evan Spiegel's decision to turn down Facebook's $3 billion offer for Snapchat in 2013 was based on his belief in the company's higher long-term value, a decision that ultimately proved correct as Snap Inc.'s market capitalization far exceeded that offer after its IPO.

Risk management is another critical aspect of financial acumen in entrepreneurship, serving as a fundamental pillar for sustaining and growing a business in unpredictable environments. Successful entrepreneurs recognize that while taking risks is inherent to entrepreneurship, managing those risks effectively can be the difference between long-term success and failure. Ray Dalio, the founder of Bridgewater Associates, is a prime example of an entrepreneur who has mastered the art of risk management. His emphasis on "radical transparency" in financial matters has allowed his hedge fund to navigate complex financial landscapes with clarity and precision. Dalio's approach involves a deep understanding of potential risks and the development of strategies to mitigate them before they escalate. This principle has not only safeguarded Bridgewater Associates but has also set a precedent for how entrepreneurs can incorporate rigorous risk management into their own ventures. Incorporating risk management into a business strategy requires a balance between bold decision-making and cautious planning. Steve Jobs, co-founder of Apple, understood the importance of this balance. While Jobs was known for his visionary leadership and willingness to take risks on groundbreaking products like the iPhone, he also recognized the need to manage financial risks to ensure the company's sustainability. Apple's meticulous attention to detail in product development, coupled with strategic financial planning, minimized the risk of failure, even as the company ventured into uncharted technological territories. As Jobs once remarked, "Innovation distinguishes between a leader and a follower," but it is the calculated management of risks that enables innovation to thrive without jeopardizing the entire enterprise.

Similarly, Jeff Bezos, founder of Amazon, has demonstrated how effective risk management can fuel exponential growth. From the early days of Amazon as an online bookstore to its evolution into a global e-commerce giant, Bezos has consistently approached risk with a strategic mindset. He recognized that while experimentation and innovation were essential for growth, they needed to be balanced with an understanding of the potential downsides. Bezos's "two-way door" decision-making framework, which allows for reversible decisions, exemplifies how entrepreneurs can take calculated risks while retaining the flexibility to pivot if necessary. This approach has enabled Amazon to explore new business ventures with confidence, knowing that risks are manageable and can be adjusted as needed.

Risk management is not just about protecting the downside but also about identifying opportunities where calculated risks can lead to significant rewards. For instance, Elon Musk's ventures into space exploration with SpaceX and electric vehicles with Tesla highlight how embracing risk, when paired with thorough research and strategic planning, can lead to groundbreaking success. Musk's willingness to invest in innovative but high-risk projects has pushed the boundaries of technology and reshaped entire industries. However, his approach is always rooted in a deep understanding of the risks involved and the potential impact on his companies. As Musk himself stated, "When something is important enough, you do it even if the odds are not in your favor." His success underscores the importance of not just managing risks but also knowing when to take them. Effective risk management extends beyond financial considerations; it encompasses the broader operational and strategic aspects of a business. For entrepreneurs like Howard Schultz, former CEO of Starbucks, managing risks involved understanding the cultural and market dynamics that could impact the company's growth. Schultz's decision to expand Starbucks globally was accompanied by careful analysis of the risks associated with entering new markets. By developing strategies to adapt to local tastes and preferences, Schultz mitigated the risk of failure and successfully transformed Starbucks into a global brand. His approach illustrates that managing risks requires a holistic view of the business environment, allowing entrepreneurs to anticipate challenges and develop proactive solutions.

Risk management is an indispensable component of financial acumen in entrepreneurship, shaping the decisions that lead to sustainable growth and innovation. Entrepreneurs like Ray Dalio, Steve Jobs, Jeff Bezos, Elon Musk, and Howard Schultz exemplify how understanding and mitigating risks can drive success, even in the most uncertain of circumstances. Their experiences remind us that while entrepreneurship involves stepping into the unknown, it is the thoughtful management of risks that turns bold visions into thriving realities. As Warren Buffett wisely observed, "Risk comes from not knowing what you're doing." Entrepreneurs who embrace risk management as a core part of their strategy are better equipped to navigate the challenges of their journey, ensuring that their ventures not only survive but also prosper in the long term.

In terms of networking and mentorship, the importance of these elements in entrepreneurial success cannot be overstated. Beyond just opening doors, strong networks provide entrepreneurs with diverse perspectives, industry insights, and potential collaborations that can be transformative for their businesses. Reid Hoffman, co-founder of LinkedIn, often speaks about the concept of "network literacy" - the ability to leverage one's network effectively. This skill involves not just building connections, but understanding how to activate and utilize these relationships in mutually beneficial ways. Mentorship, as highlighted by Oprah Winfrey's experience, can provide invaluable guidance at all stages of an entrepreneur's journey. Mentors can offer not just advice, but also emotional support, which is crucial given the often-isolating nature of entrepreneurship. They can help entrepreneurs avoid common pitfalls, make strategic decisions, and provide introductions to key players in their industry. For example, Steve Jobs famously mentored Mark Zuckerberg during Facebook's early days, offering crucial advice on team building and company vision.

The concept of "giving before you get" is increasingly recognized as a powerful networking strategy in entrepreneurship. This approach, advocated by Adam Grant in his book "Give and Take," suggests that entrepreneurs who focus on adding value to their networks rather than just extracting benefits often end up more successful in the long run. This mindset fosters stronger, more authentic relationships that can yield unexpected opportunities and support.

While innovation and creativity are often celebrated as the hallmarks of successful entrepreneurship, financial acumen and strong networks are equally crucial components. They provide the foundation and support structure that allow innovative ideas to flourish and scale. As entrepreneurs navigate the complex journey to prosperity, mastering these skills can make the difference between a good idea and a successful, sustainable business.

While entrepreneurship demands significant time and energy, the pursuit of work-life balance is essential not only for personal well-being but also for sustaining long-term business success. Entrepreneurs who integrate balance into their lives are often more resilient, creative, and effective in their roles, as they can draw upon the strength and stability that come from nurturing all aspects of their lives. Arianna Huffington, co-founder of The Huffington Post, is a vocal proponent of prioritizing well-being in the entrepreneurial journey. After collapsing from exhaustion in 2007, she realized that the relentless drive for success at the expense of health and relationships was unsustainable. This experience led her to launch Thrive Global, a platform dedicated to improving well-being and performance by encouraging a healthier work-life balance. As Huffington often emphasizes, "We need to redefine success beyond money and power to include well-being, wisdom, and our ability to wonder and give back." Entrepreneurs who maintain a balanced life are often better decision-makers. By taking time to disconnect from work, they gain fresh perspectives and can approach challenges with renewed energy. This principle is exemplified by Bill Gates, who famously takes "Think Weeks" twice a year, during which he retreats to a secluded location to read, reflect, and plan. These breaks not only allow him to recharge but also contribute to his ability to think strategically and innovate consistently. Gates's practice underscores the idea that time away from work can be as crucial to success as the time spent working. Additionally, fostering a balanced lifestyle can enhance creativity, which is vital for entrepreneurial innovation. Walt Disney, the visionary behind The Walt Disney Company, understood the importance of leisure and personal time in fueling creativity. Disney would often retreat to his favorite hobby of model train building, where he found relaxation and inspiration away from the demands of running a business. This downtime allowed him to return to his work with fresh ideas and the creative energy needed to build his entertainment empire. Disney's approach demonstrates how personal interests and hobbies can serve as a wellspring of inspiration, directly benefiting business outcomes. The concept of balance extends beyond the individual entrepreneur to the organizational culture they create. Leaders who value work-life balance tend to cultivate healthier, more motivated teams. Satya Nadella, CEO of Microsoft, has championed a culture of empathy and flexibility at the company, recognizing that employees who feel supported in their personal lives are more engaged and productive. Under Nadella's leadership, Microsoft has introduced policies that promote work-life balance, such as flexible working hours and mental health support, which have contributed to the company's innovation and success. As Nadella asserts, "Empathy makes you a better innovator," reflecting how a balanced, supportive work environment can lead to greater business achievements. Maintaining a healthy work-life balance is not merely a personal choice but a strategic business decision. Entrepreneurs who prioritize their well-being, along with the well-being of their teams, create a foundation for sustainable success. Whether through personal practices like those of Arianna Huffington and Bill Gates or through fostering supportive organizational cultures like Satya Nadella, the integration of work-life balance can lead to more creative, resilient, and ultimately more prosperous business endeavors. As these examples illustrate, true

success in entrepreneurship lies not just in the pursuit of financial goals, but in achieving a holistic balance that supports both personal fulfillment and professional excellence.

True prosperity in entrepreneurship extends beyond personal wealth, involving a dedication to making a positive impact on society. Many successful entrepreneurs leverage their resources and influence to give back, whether through philanthropy, social enterprises, or ethical business practices. This commitment not only builds a lasting legacy but also significantly enhances the well-being of others. Muhammad Yunus, founder of Grameen Bank, is a prime example of using entrepreneurial success to address global challenges. His pioneering work in microfinance, providing small loans to those without access to traditional banking, has empowered millions to improve their lives and build sustainable businesses. Yunus's approach illustrates how entrepreneurship can address systemic issues and foster economic development. His belief in the power of social business aligns with the biblical principle from Luke 12:48, "To whom much is given, much is expected," as he has channeled his success into uplifting others.

Another notable example is Richard Branson, founder of the Virgin Group, who integrates philanthropy into his business ethos through Virgin Unite, the nonprofit arm of his company. Virgin Unite supports various causes, including entrepreneurial development in emerging markets and climate change initiatives. Branson's efforts reflect a broader understanding of prosperity, where business success is intertwined with a commitment to addressing social challenges. He has observed, "The more you give, the more you receive," emphasizing how contributing to societal well-being enhances both personal fulfillment and business success.

Blake Mycoskie, the founder of TOMS Shoes, demonstrates how embedding social responsibility into business models can yield significant benefits. His "One for One" model, which ensures that each pair of shoes sold results in a pair being donated to a child in need, effectively addresses social issues while driving business success. Mycoskie's approach illustrates that entrepreneurial ventures can achieve both financial success and meaningful social impact, embodying the idea that prosperity is most fulfilling when it serves a greater purpose.

, Howard Schultz, former CEO of Starbucks, exemplifies how social responsibility can be integral to business strategy. Schultz's commitment to ethical sourcing, employee welfare, and community engagement has helped shape Starbucks into a company known for its corporate social responsibility. His focus on creating positive change through business practices reflects the belief that true prosperity involves contributing to the greater good. Schultz's approach to leadership and philanthropy is captured in his view that "Success is not about the accumulation of wealth; it's about creating value for society."

True prosperity in entrepreneurship is characterized by a commitment to making a positive impact on society. Entrepreneurs like Muhammad Yunus, Richard Branson, Blake Mycoskie, and Howard Schultz show that using one's success to address social issues not only creates a lasting legacy but also enriches the lives of many. Their actions embody the biblical principle from Luke 12:48, demonstrating that genuine success is achieved when personal wealth is aligned with efforts to better the world. Prosperity, in this context, is defined not just by financial gain but by the meaningful contributions one can make through their entrepreneurial endeavors. Entrepreneurship is a rewarding path to prosperity, offering the freedom to innovate, the opportunity to create lasting wealth, and the ability to make a meaningful impact on the world. While the journey is filled with challenges, those who embrace it with passion, resilience, and a commitment to continuous growth can achieve remarkable success. Steve Jobs captured the essence of this journey when he said, "The only way to do great work is to love what you do." As you embark on your entrepreneurial journey, remember that your path to prosperity is within reach. Embrace it with confidence and determination, and take the first step today.

Chapter 5. Embracing Entrepreneurship as a Path to Prosperity

Reflective Questions

1. What personal strengths do I possess that could contribute to my success as an entrepreneur?

2. How does my definition of prosperity align with the goals I have set for my entrepreneurial journey?

3. What challenges or fears do I need to overcome to fully embrace entrepreneurship as a path to prosperity?

4. In what ways can I leverage my passion and skills to create a business that not only prospers financially but also fulfills my personal mission?

5. How can I ensure that my entrepreneurial endeavors contribute positively to my community and align with my values of ethics and integrity?

6. What steps can I take to build resilience and adaptability as I navigate the uncertainties of entrepreneurship?

7. How can I balance the pursuit of financial prosperity with maintaining a healthy work-life balance and well-being?

8. What resources, networks, or mentors can I seek out to support my entrepreneurial growth and success?

9. How do I measure success in my entrepreneurial journey beyond financial gain, and what milestones will indicate progress toward my broader goals?

10. What long-term vision do I have for my business, and how does it align with my aspirations for prosperity, both personally and professionally?

Chapter 6:
The Power of Strategic Investing

This is the section of the book where I must acknowledge that I am not an expert in investing. While I do invest in the stock market, my approach is that of a social and conscientious investor. I focus on businesses that align with my values and beliefs, ensuring that my investments do not support practices contrary to my principles. For example, I would not invest in a company that opposes providing aid to single parents or children. As a realtor, some of my investments are in real estate investment trusts (REITs) and commercial real estate. Additionally, as the founder of a nonprofit, I invest in cause-related opportunities, such as affordable housing.

Before we delve into Strategic Investing, I want to share pre-investing recommendations, such as ensuring your financial foundation is solid so your investments can grow without being jeopardized by unexpected financial needs. One of the first steps is to focus on paying down high-interest debt, such as credit card balances, as these obligations can quickly cause A loss of any gains made from investing. Eliminating or significantly reducing this debt not only frees up cash flow but also minimizes financial stress, allowing you to invest more confidently. You should also build an emergency fund by saving at least three to six months' worth of living expenses that are easily accessible in the event of an unforeseen circumstance. Once these foundational steps are in place, you can begin investing and concentrating on your long-term financial goals.

Investing is more than just a means to grow wealth; it's a strategic tool that, when used effectively, can positively affect the trajectory of your financial future and empower you to achieve your long-term goals. Strategic investing is about making informed decisions, guided by a deep understanding of market dynamics, risk tolerance, and personal objectives. As Warren Buffett, one of the most successful investors of all time, famously said, "Risk comes from not knowing what you're doing." This quote summarizes the meaning of strategic investing: knowledge and planning reduce risk and enhance the likelihood of success. Strategic investments are made by individuals or companies with the goal of gaining an edge in the market, growing over the long term, and earning solid financial returns. These investments are carefully chosen to align with bigger goals, whether for a business or personal financial plan.

The first step in strategic investing is understanding your financial goals. Are you saving for retirement, building a college fund for your children, or accumulating wealth for a major purchase like a home or a business venture? Each goal will dictate a different investment strategy. For instance, if you're saving for retirement decades away, you might opt for a more aggressive strategy with a higher allocation to stocks, which historically have provided higher

returns over the long term. If your goal is short-term, like buying a home within five years, a more conservative approach with bonds or cash equivalents might be appropriate. Take the example of a young professional named Sarah, who started investing in her late twenties. Sarah's goal was to retire early and travel the world. She understood that achieving this would require a robust investment strategy. Sarah began by maxing out her contributions to her 401(k) and Roth IRA, both of which provided tax advantages that would help her money grow more efficiently. She then diversified her portfolio with a mix of domestic and international stocks, bonds, and real estate investment trusts (REITs). By taking advantage of compounding returns, Sarah was on track to achieve her goal by her early fifties.

Diversification is another key principle of strategic investing. "Don't put all your eggs in one basket" is a timeless adage that applies perfectly to investing. Diversification involves spreading your investments across various asset classes, such as stocks, bonds, real estate, and commodities to reduce risk. If one investment strategy underperforms, the others can help mitigate the impact on your overall portfolio. This strategy is particularly important in uncertain or volatile markets. For instance, during the 2008 financial crisis, investors with diversified portfolios were better able to weather the storm compared to those heavily invested in a single sector, such as real estate or financial services. Let's consider the case of John, a middle-aged investor with a high-risk tolerance. John had a significant portion of his portfolio invested in technology stocks, which were performing exceptionally well in the early 2000s. John's experience with the dot-com bubble burst and his subsequent investment strategy adjustment serves as a prime example of effective risk management in action. When the tech sector crashed, John's concentrated portfolio suffered significant losses, highlighting the dangers of overexposure to a single industry. Recognizing this vulnerability, he wisely diversified his investments across various asset classes, including bonds, real estate, and international stocks. This strategic shift not only helped stabilize his portfolio against future market shocks but also positioned him to capitalize on growth opportunities in different sectors. By adapting his approach and embracing diversification, John demonstrated key risk management principles: assessing and mitigating risks, maintaining a balance between potential returns and stability, and taking a long-term perspective on wealth building. His ability to learn from the market downturn and adjust his strategy accordingly showcases the importance of flexibility and continuous reassessment in managing investment risks. Through this prudent approach to risk management, John was able to create a more resilient portfolio better equipped to navigate the complexities and uncertainties of the financial markets. Risk management is a critical component of strategic investing. Every investment carries some level of risk, and understanding how to manage that risk is essential for long-term success. One effective way to manage risk is through asset allocation, which involves dividing your investments among different asset categories based on your risk tolerance, financial goals, and investment horizon. For example, younger investors with a longer time horizon may allocate a larger portion of their portfolio to stocks, which, while more volatile, offer the potential for higher returns. On the other hand, older investors nearing retirement might prefer a more conservative allocation with a higher percentage of bonds or fixed-income securities.

Another powerful tool in strategic investing is dollar-cost averaging, a technique where you invest a fixed amount of money at regular intervals, regardless of market conditions. This strategy helps mitigate the impact of market volatility by averaging the cost of your investments over time. For instance, if you invest $500 monthly in a mutual fund, you'll buy more shares when prices are low and fewer shares when prices are high. Over time, this can lead to a lower average cost per share and reduce the impact of market fluctuations on your portfolio. Consider the example of Emily, a new investor who started her investment journey during a period of market volatility. Instead of trying to time the market, Emily opted for dollar-cost averaging by investing $200 every month in a diversified index fund. This approach allowed her to steadily build her portfolio, taking advantage of lower prices during market dips. Over the years, Emily's consistent investing, combined with the power of compounding, helped her grow her wealth significantly. Strategic investing also involves regular portfolio reviews and rebalancing. As markets fluctuate and investments grow at different rates, your portfolio's asset allocation may drift from its original target. Rebalancing involves periodically adjusting your portfolio to realign with your desired asset allocation. For instance, if your target allocation is 60% stocks and 40% bonds, but due to strong market performance, your stock allocation has grown to 70%, rebalancing would involve selling some stocks and buying bonds to bring the allocation back in line. This disciplined approach helps maintain your risk level and ensures that your portfolio remains aligned with your investment goals.

Strategic investing isn't merely about accumulating wealth; it's equally about preserving it, ensuring that the hard-earned gains are not diminished by unforeseen circumstances. As your portfolio grows, implementing protective measures becomes crucial to shield your assets from potential risks, such as market downturns, inflation, and unexpected expenses. For instance, diversifying into inflation-protected securities, like Treasury Inflation-Protected Securities (TIPS), can be a prudent strategy. TIPS are designed to protect your investment from the diminishing effects of inflation by adjusting their principal value in line with changes in the Consumer Price Index (CPI). This means that as inflation rises, the value of TIPS increases, helping to maintain your purchasing power over time. Warren Buffett once emphasized, "The first rule of investing is don't lose money; the second rule is don't forget rule number one." This mindset underscores the importance of not just making money but also ensuring that your wealth is safeguarded against risks. Maintaining an emergency fund is another critical component of a well-rounded investment strategy. This fund acts as a financial buffer, allowing you to cover unexpected expenses or ride out market downturns without the need to liquidate investments at an inopportune time. Selling assets during a market dip could lock in losses and potentially derail your long-term financial plan. For example, during the 2008 financial crisis, many investors who lacked sufficient liquidity were forced to sell at the bottom of the market, turning paper losses into real ones. By contrast, those with an emergency fund could weather the storm, allowing their investments to recover over time. Strategic investing is about the long game—building wealth while simultaneously protecting it against the inevitable bumps along the road.

A prime example of strategic wealth preservation is reflected in the investment approach adopted by many retirees, who often transition from a growth-focused strategy to one centered on income generation and capital preservation. As retirement approaches, the need to secure a stable income and protect accumulated wealth becomes paramount. This shift might involve reallocating assets from growth-oriented stocks to income-generating investments like dividend-paying stocks, bonds, and annuities. For example, consider a retiree with a $1 million portfolio. They might allocate a significant portion to high-quality dividend-paying stocks, such as those from established companies with a history of consistent payouts. This strategy can provide a steady stream of income, which is crucial for covering living expenses in retirement. At the same time, the retiree might invest the remainder in bonds, particularly government or high-grade corporate bonds, to preserve capital and reduce exposure to market volatility. This balanced approach not only helps to ensure a reliable income stream but also mitigates the risk of significant losses, which can be particularly detrimental in the post-retirement phase when there's less time to recover from market downturns. As financial advisor Benjamin Graham once advised, "The essence of investment management is the management of risks, not the management of returns." This perspective underscores the importance of capital preservation as a key element of strategic wealth management, especially for those in retirement. Additionally, some retirees might consider annuities, which can provide guaranteed income for life, further reducing the risk of outliving their savings. By carefully selecting and combining these income-generating and capital-preserving investments, retirees can create a robust financial plan that supports their lifestyle while safeguarding their wealth for the future. This approach exemplifies how strategic wealth preservation can be tailored to meet the unique needs of those in retirement, ensuring financial stability and peace of mind.

Strategic investing involves creating a well-balanced portfolio to achieve long-term financial goals while managing risk. A crucial component of this strategy is understanding and utilizing bonds effectively. Bonds are essentially loans that investors make to governments or corporations, receiving regular interest payments and the return of the principal at maturity.

Bond Types

1. Government bonds: These are considered among the safest investments. U.S. Treasury bonds, for example, are backed by the full faith and credit of the U.S. government. They typically offer lower yields but provide stability to a portfolio. For

instance, a 10-year Treasury note might yield around 1.5% to 3%, depending on economic conditions.

2. Corporate bonds: These are issued by companies to raise capital. They generally offer higher yields than government bonds but come with more risk. For example, a high-quality corporate bond (investment grade) might yield 3-5%, while a lower-quality bond (high yield or "junk" bond) could offer yields of 7% or more.

3. Municipal bonds: Issued by state and local governments, these bonds often provide tax advantages. Their yields might be lower than corporate bonds, but the tax benefits can make them attractive to investors in higher tax brackets.

4. Treasury Inflation-Protected Securities (TIPS): These government bonds adjust with inflation, protecting purchasing power. While the base yield might be low (even negative at times), the principal increases with inflation.

Bonds play several important roles in a portfolio:

1. Income generation: Bonds provide regular interest payments, which can be particularly valuable for retirees or those seeking steady income.

2. Capital preservation: High-quality bonds tend to be less volatile than stocks, helping to preserve capital during market downturns.

3. Diversification: Bonds often move differently from stocks, helping to smooth out portfolio returns. As investor Ray Dalio notes, "Diversifying well is the most important thing you need to do in order to invest well."

4. Risk management: By adjusting the ratio of stocks to bonds, investors can control their portfolio's overall risk level. A classic rule of thumb suggests subtracting your age from 100 to determine the percentage of stocks in your portfolio, with the remainder in bonds.

When investing in bonds, it's important to consider factors such as duration (a measure of interest rate sensitivity) and credit quality. Longer-duration bonds are more sensitive to interest rate changes, while lower credit quality bonds carry more default risk but offer higher yields. Investors can access bonds through individual purchases, bond mutual funds, or exchange-traded funds (ETFs). For many investors, a low-cost, broadly diversified bond fund or ETF can provide easy access to the benefits of bonds without the complexity of managing individual bonds. Remember, while bonds are generally considered less risky than stocks, they still carry risks. Interest rate risk (bond prices fall when interest rates rise), credit risk (risk of default), and inflation risk (eroding purchasing power) are all important considerations. As with all investments, it's crucial to align your bond strategy with your overall financial goals, risk tolerance, and investment timeline. As investment legend Benjamin Graham advised, "The essence of investment management is the management of risks, not the management of returns."

Strategic investing is indeed a powerful approach to building long-term wealth and financial security. Let's delve deeper into the key components of this strategy and how they work together to create a robust investment plan.

Setting clear objectives is the foundation of strategic investing. This involves defining specific, measurable financial goals, such as saving for retirement, funding your children's education, or building a nest egg for a major purchase. As Peter Lynch, the legendary fund manager, once said, "Know what you own, and know why you own it." This clarity of purpose guides all subsequent investment decisions.

Diversification is a cornerstone of strategic investing. By spreading investments across various asset classes, sectors, and geographic regions, you can reduce the impact of poor performance in any single area. For example, a diversified portfolio might include:

1. Domestic stocks for growth potential

2. International stocks for global exposure

3. Bonds for income and stability

4. Real estate investment trusts (REITs) for property market exposure

5. Commodities or precious metals as a hedge against inflation

Warren Buffett cautions against over-diversification, however, stating, "Diversification is protection against ignorance. It makes little sense if you know what you are doing." The key is to find the right balance that aligns with your knowledge and risk tolerance. Risk management is crucial in strategic investing. This involves not only diversifying but also understanding and controlling the level of risk in your portfolio. One common approach is adjusting your asset allocation based on your age and risk tolerance. For instance, a young investor might have a portfolio with 80% stocks and 20% bonds, while a retiree might reverse that ratio. As John Bogle, founder of Vanguard, advised, "Your success in investing will depend in part on your character and guts, and in part on your ability to realize at the height of ebullience and the depth of despair alike that this too shall pass." Regular portfolio review and rebalancing are essential components of strategic investing. Market movements can shift your asset allocation away from your target percentages. Rebalancing involves selling some of your best-performing assets and buying more of the underperforming ones to maintain your desired asset mix. This disciplined approach helps you "buy low and sell high" automatically. Continuous education is vital in strategic investing. Markets evolve, new investment vehicles emerge, and economic conditions change. Staying informed allows you to adapt your strategy as needed. As Ray Dalio, founder of Bridgewater Associates, says, "The biggest mistake investors make is to believe that what happened in the recent past is likely to persist." Cost management is another crucial aspect of strategic investing. High fees can significantly erode returns over time. Utilizing low-cost index funds or ETFs for the core of your portfolio can help minimize expenses. Jack Bogle emphasized this point, stating, "The miracle of compounding returns is overwhelmed by the tyranny of compounding costs." Patience and discipline are perhaps the most challenging yet important elements of strategic investing. It's easy to be swayed by market volatility or the latest investment fad. However, successful strategic investors maintain a long-term perspective. As Warren Buffett famously said, "The stock market is a device for transferring money from the impatient to the patient." Lastly, consider seeking professional advice, especially for complex financial situations. A financial advisor can help refine your strategy, provide objective insights, and keep you accountable to your plan.

Remember, strategic investing is not about finding a get-rich-quick scheme or timing the market perfectly. It's about creating a thoughtful, personalized plan and sticking to it through market ups and downs. As Christopher Davis aptly put it, "You make most of your money in a bear market, you just don't realize it at the time." By following these principles of strategic investing, you can build a robust portfolio designed to weather market volatility and help you achieve your long-term financial goals.

Chapter 7:
Financial Literacy and Empowerment

Financial literacy and empowerment are crucial skills in today's complex economic landscape. They provide individuals with the knowledge, tools, and confidence to make informed decisions about their money, ultimately leading to greater financial security and freedom. This comprehensive guide will explore the various aspects of financial literacy and empowerment, with a particular focus on credit, debt, and insurance. At its core, financial literacy is the ability to understand and effectively use various financial skills, including personal financial management, budgeting, and making informed decisions about credit and insurance. It's about having the knowledge and confidence to navigate the complex world of personal finance. Financial literacy encompasses a wide range of topics from basic money management to understanding complex financial products and services. The importance of financial literacy cannot be overstated. In an increasingly complex financial world, being financially literate can mean the difference between struggling to make ends meet and achieving financial stability. It empowers individuals to take control of their financial lives, make smart decisions, and protect themselves from financial pitfalls. Financial literacy begins with understanding basic concepts such as income, expenses, savings, and debt. It involves learning how to create and stick to a budget, how to save for short-term and long-term goals, and how to use credit responsibly. As your knowledge grows, you can delve into more advanced topics like insurance products, retirement planning, and tax strategies. A solid understanding of financial literacy lays the foundation for sound money management, and one of the key pillars in this journey is creating and maintaining a budget.

The journey to financial empowerment begins with building a strong financial foundation, and this foundation starts with creating a budget. A budget is essentially a plan for how you will spend and save your money, acting as a financial roadmap that helps you understand where your money is going and allows you to make informed decisions about your spending. To create an effective budget, start by tracking all of your income and expenses for a month. This process should be both honest and thorough, capturing every dollar that comes in and goes out. With a clear picture of your financial situation, you can then make strategic decisions about where to cut back on spending and where you might be able to save more. One of the most crucial components of any budget is the inclusion of an emergency fund. This fund is a savings account specifically set aside to cover unexpected expenses or financial emergencies, such as medical bills, car repairs, or job loss. Financial experts commonly recommend that an emergency fund contain three to six months' worth of living expenses. This range provides a sufficient safety net to cover your basic needs during periods of financial instability without needing to rely on high-interest debt, such as credit cards or personal loans. For example, if your monthly living expenses total $3,000, your emergency fund should ideally be between $9,000 and $18,000. Calculating the amount needed for your emergency fund involves taking a close look at your essential monthly expenses. Start by listing your non-negotiable costs, such as rent or mortgage payments, utilities, groceries, insurance, and minimum debt payments. Multiply this total by the number of months you want your emergency fund to cover. For instance, if your essential monthly expenses amount to $2,500, and you aim to save six months' worth, you would need $15,000 in your emergency fund. Building this fund may take time, but consistency is key. Even setting aside a small amount each month can gradually build up your emergency savings. Dave Ramsey, a well-known financial advisor, emphasizes, "Save $1,000 as a starter emergency fund and then work towards three to six months of expenses." This advice highlights the importance of starting with a manageable goal and progressively building up your financial safety net. To make saving for your emergency fund more manageable, consider automating your savings. Set up a direct deposit from your paycheck into a designated savings account so that you consistently contribute to your fund without the temptation to spend that money elsewhere. This approach ensures that your emergency savings grow steadily over time, providing peace of mind and financial security. It's important to keep your emergency fund in a separate, easily accessible account, such as a high-yield savings account, rather than in investments that fluctuate in value or are difficult to liquidate quickly. The purpose of an emergency fund is to be there when you need it most, without the risk of losing value or facing penalties for early withdrawal. Suze Orman, a financial guru, advises, "An emergency fund is like a security blanket. It's your protection against the unexpected, and it gives you the confidence to face whatever comes your way." By incorporating an emergency fund into your budget, you create a financial buffer that allows you to weather life's unexpected challenges without derailing your long-term financial goals. It's a vital step in achieving financial empowerment, ensuring that you are prepared for the unexpected and can maintain financial stability even in difficult times.

Credit and debt are integral components of most people's financial lives, with the power to either facilitate financial growth or create significant obstacles to financial freedom. When managed wisely, credit can be a powerful tool for achieving financial goals, such as purchasing a home, financing education, or managing business cash flow. However, mismanaged debt can lead to financial difficulties, affecting everything from your ability to secure loans to your overall financial stability. Understanding how credit works is essential for navigating these complexities and making informed financial decisions. This includes knowing how credit scores are calculated, what factors affect your creditworthiness, and how to build and maintain good credit.

Your credit score is a numerical representation of your creditworthiness, typically ranging from 300 to 850. The higher your score, the more likely you are to be approved for loans and credit cards with favorable terms. This score is calculated by the three major credit bureaus: Experian, Equifax, and TransUnion.

These agencies collect and maintain credit information on millions of consumers, which lenders use to assess the risk of lending to you. Your credit score is primarily influenced by five key factors:

1. Payment History (35% of your score): This is the most significant factor in your credit score. It tracks whether you've paid your bills on time, including credit cards, loans, mortgages, and any other lines of credit. A history of late payments, defaults, or accounts sent to collections can significantly lower your score.

2. Credit Utilization Ratio (30%): This measures how much of your available credit you're using at any given time. It's calculated by dividing your total credit card balances by your total credit card limits. Ideally, you should aim to keep your credit utilization below 30%, as higher utilization can indicate higher risk to lenders.

3. Length of Credit History (15%): The longer your credit history, the better. This factor considers the age of your oldest account, the age of your newest account, and the average age of all your accounts. A longer credit history provides more data for lenders to assess your creditworthiness.

4. Types of Credit Accounts (10%): Having a mix of credit types, such as credit cards, installment loans, mortgages, and retail accounts, can positively affect your score. It shows lenders that you can manage different types of credit responsibly.

5. Recent Credit Inquiries (10%): Each time you apply for new credit, a hard inquiry is recorded on your credit report. Multiple recent inquiries can negatively impact your score, as they may signal that you're taking on new debt.

High credit scores typically result from consistent, on-time payments, low credit utilization, a long credit history, and a diverse mix of credit accounts. Conversely, low credit scores can result from late or missed payments, high credit utilization, a short credit history, and frequent credit inquiries. Negative items, such as bankruptcies, foreclosures, and accounts in collections, can also severely impact your credit score and may remain on your credit report for years.

Understanding how long items stay on your credit report is crucial for managing your credit health. Most negative information, such as late payments and charge-offs, remains on your credit report for seven years from the date of the first delinquency. Bankruptcies can stay on your report for up to 10 years, depending on the type. However, positive information, like accounts paid as agreed, can remain on your credit report indefinitely, serving as a testament to your creditworthiness. This highlights the importance of consistently monitoring your credit to ensure that both positive and negative items are accurately reflected in your report. By staying vigilant with credit monitoring, you can track the progress of your financial habits, promptly identify any discrepancies, and protect your credit from potential errors or fraudulent activity.

If you discover incorrect information on your credit report, it's essential to take steps to correct it as soon as possible. Errors can occur, and they can have a significant impact on your credit score. The Fair Credit Reporting Act (FCRA) gives you the right to dispute any inaccurate or incomplete information in your credit report. To delete incorrect credit information, start by obtaining a copy of your credit report from each of the three major credit bureaus. You're entitled to a free report from each bureau annually, which you can request at [AnnualCreditReport.com] (https://www.annualcreditreport.com). If you find an error, such as a payment marked late when it was actually on time, or an account you don't recognize, you can dispute it with the credit bureau that reported the error. This process typically involves submitting a dispute online or by mail, providing documentation that supports your claim. The credit bureau is then required to investigate the dispute, usually within 30 days. If the bureau finds that the information is indeed incorrect, it must correct the error and provide you with a free updated credit report. In addition to monitoring your credit, it's important to safeguard your credit and protect yourself from identity theft. Identity theft occurs when someone uses your personal information, such as your Social Security number, credit card number, or bank account information, without your permission. This can result in fraudulent accounts, unauthorized charges, and significant damage to your credit score. To avoid identity theft, follow these best practices:

1. Monitor Your Credit Regularly: Use services like [Credit Karma] (https://www.creditkarma.com), [Experian](https://www.experian.com), or [Equifax](https://www.equifax.com) to monitor your credit report regularly. These services often provide free credit monitoring, alerts for any significant changes to your report, and tools to help you understand your credit score.

2. Use Strong, Unique Passwords: Protect your online financial accounts with strong, unique passwords. Avoid using easily guessable information, like your name or birthdate, and consider using a password manager to keep track of your passwords securely.

3. Enable Two-Factor Authentication (2FA): Where possible, enable two-factor authentication on your financial accounts. This adds an extra layer of security by requiring a second form of verification, such as a text message code, in addition to your password.

4. Be Cautious with Personal Information: Avoid sharing your personal information, such as your Social Security number or credit card information, over the phone or online unless you're sure of the recipient's identity. Be wary of phishing emails or phone calls that attempt to trick you into revealing personal details.

5. Shred Sensitive Documents: Before discarding any documents that contain personal information, such as bank

statements or credit card offers, shred them to prevent thieves from retrieving your information from the trash.

6. Consider Freezing Your Credit: A credit freeze restricts access to your credit report, making it more difficult for identity thieves to open new accounts in your name. You can freeze your credit for free through each of the major credit bureaus.

It's important to know that not everything goes on your credit report. For example, your income, bank account balances, and utility payments generally do not affect your credit score. However, if you fail to pay your utility bills or rent, and the account is sent to a collection agency, that negative information can be reported to the credit bureaus and impact your score. Similarly, soft inquiries, such as when you check your own credit or when a lender pre-approves you for a loan, do not affect your credit score.

Understanding credit and how it impacts your financial life is an essential part of financial literacy. A good credit score can open doors to lower interest rates and better financial opportunities, while a poor credit score can limit your options and increase your costs. By managing your credit wisely—through timely payments, responsible use of credit, regular monitoring of your credit reports, and safeguarding your personal information—you can build and maintain a strong credit profile. Remember, credit is a powerful tool, and with the right knowledge and habits, you can use it to achieve your financial goals and secure your financial future.

To maintain a good credit score:

1. Pay all bills on time

2. Keep credit card balances low

3. Don't close old credit accounts unnecessarily

4. Limit new credit applications

5. Regularly check your credit report for errors

Understanding the distinction between good debt and bad debt is essential for effective financial stewardship. Good debt can be likened to a wise investment that yields positive returns over time, similar to the principles found in Proverbs 21:20, which says, "The wise store up choice food and olive oil, but fools gulp theirs down." This scripture highlights the importance of wise management and preparation, akin to taking on low-interest debt for purposes that increase your net worth or future earning potential. For example, a mortgage on a home that appreciates in value or student loans that lead to a higher income can be considered good debt. These types of debt are often seen as investments in your future, reflecting the wisdom of careful planning. Consider a scenario where you take out a mortgage to purchase a home. Over time, as the home appreciates in value, you build equity, effectively increasing your net worth. This aligns with the principle in Proverbs 24:3-4: "By wisdom a house is built, and through understanding it is established; through knowledge its rooms are filled with rare and beautiful treasures." Similarly, student loans, while a burden, are often seen as good debt because they fund education, which typically results in higher lifetime earnings. As Ecclesiastes 7:12 reminds us, "Wisdom is a shelter as money is a shelter, but the advantage of knowledge is this: Wisdom preserves those who have it." The investment in education through student loans is an investment in wisdom, which ultimately shelters and preserves. On the other hand, bad debt is comparable to the foolishness warned against in Proverbs 22:7: "The rich rule over the poor, and the borrower is slave to the lender." Bad debt is often high-interest debt used to fund consumption rather than investment, such as credit card debt, which typically carries high interest rates. For example, using a credit card to finance a vacation or purchase luxury items can lead to financial enslavement, as interest compounds and the debt becomes increasingly difficult to manage. In this context, Proverbs 22:26-27 advises, "Do not be one who shakes hands in pledge or puts up security for debts; if you lack the means to pay, your very bed will be snatched from under you." If you find yourself in a situation where you are struggling to manage debt, it is vital to approach the matter with wisdom and diligence, as guided by the teachings in Proverbs 6:1-5, which encourage resolving debts quickly to avoid being ensnared. This is where communication with debt collectors comes into play. Knowing when and how to communicate with them can prevent further complications. The first step is to ensure that you understand your rights, as Proverbs 2:6-7 suggests seeking knowledge and discretion: "For the Lord gives wisdom; from His mouth come knowledge and understanding. He holds success in store for the upright, He is a shield to those whose walk is blameless."

When dealing with debt collectors, it is essential to communicate in writing to document your interactions and protect your rights. This approach is supported by the biblical principle in Proverbs 4:7: "The beginning of wisdom is this: Get wisdom. Though it cost all you have, get understanding." Requesting validation of the debt in writing ensures that any claims made by the collector are substantiated. Under the Fair Debt Collection Practices Act (FDCPA), a debt collector must provide a validation of the debt within five days of initial contact. If they fail to respond within this timeframe, they are required to cease collection activities until they provide the necessary documentation. If a debt collector does not provide the required validation, you have the right to dispute the debt and request its removal from your credit report. This principle aligns with Proverbs 18:13: "To answer before listening—that is folly and shame," emphasizing the importance of receiving and reviewing all information before proceeding. Sending this letter via certified mail with a return receipt is advisable to ensure there is a record of your request and its receipt date. If the debt collector does not comply, consider filing a complaint with the Consumer Financial Protection Bureau (CFPB) or seeking legal advice. By managing your debts responsibly and understanding your rights, you can avoid the pitfalls of unresolved debt. This approach reflects the wisdom of Proverbs 21:5: "The plans of the diligent lead to profit as surely as haste leads to poverty," demonstrating the benefits of diligence and informed decision-making in financial matters.

To avoid falling into collections, judgments, or liens, it is essential to address your debts proactively. Ecclesiastes 5:5 reminds us, "It is better not to make a vow than to make one and not fulfill it." If you foresee difficulties in making payments, communicate with your creditors before the situation escalates. This proactive approach is in line with the wisdom found in Proverbs 16:3: "Commit to the Lord whatever you do, and He will establish your plans." By committing to responsible debt management, you can avoid the severe consequences of judgments and liens, which can have long-lasting impacts on your financial health. Finally, to avoid the negative consequences of unpaid debt, such as judgments and liens, follow the guidance of Proverbs 22:3: "The prudent see danger and take refuge, but the simple keep going and pay the penalty." This means maintaining open lines of communication with your creditors, settling debts before they reach the point of legal action, and seeking counsel if necessary.

Embracing the wisdom found in Hebrew scriptures can guide you in understanding the difference between good and bad debt, and in managing your debts with integrity and prudence. By borrowing wisely, staying informed, and addressing debt issues promptly, you can avoid the pitfalls of bad debt and work toward achieving true financial freedom, as emphasized in Proverbs 22:4: "Humility is the fear of the Lord; its wages are riches and honor and life. According to the U.S. Bureau of Labor Statistics, individuals with a bachelor's degree earn nearly 65% more than those with only a high school diploma. On the other hand, bad debt is often high-interest debt used to purchase depreciating assets or to fund consumption rather than investment. Credit card debt is a common example of bad debt, largely due to its high interest rates, which can quickly escalate the amount owed if not managed properly. For example, using a credit card to finance a vacation or buy the latest gadget often leads to paying significantly more than the original price due to interest. Personal finance author Suze Orman warns, "Credit card debt is the most damaging kind of debt because it carries high-interest rates, and if you're only making minimum payments, it could take decades to pay off a relatively small balance." Avoiding bad debt is crucial, but if you find yourself in a situation where you're struggling to manage debt, communication with debt collectors becomes important. It's essential to know when and how to communicate with them to avoid further complications. If you start receiving calls from debt collectors, the first step is to ensure you understand your rights under the Fair Debt Collection Practices Act (FDCPA). This federal law protects consumers from abusive practices by debt collectors and allows you to dispute the debt if you believe there has been a mistake.

When communicating with debt collectors, it's best to do so in writing. This creates a record of your interactions and ensures that your rights are protected. Start by requesting a validation of the debt, which the collector is legally obligated to provide within five days of contacting you. This letter should include details about the debt, such as the amount owed and the original creditor. If you find that the debt is accurate, you can negotiate a payment plan that fits your budget. In some cases, you may even be able to settle the debt for less than the full amount owed. For example, if you owe $5,000, the collector may agree to accept a lump sum payment of $3,500 to close the account. It's important to communicate with debt collectors promptly to avoid the situation escalating to collections, judgments, or liens. Ignoring debt collectors can lead to a lawsuit, and if the court rules in favor of the creditor, a judgment may be issued against you. This can result in wage garnishment, a lien on your property, or a bank account levy. To avoid this, be proactive in addressing your debts. If you're unable to pay, explain your situation to the collector and attempt to work out a manageable payment plan.

Avoiding collections altogether starts with managing your debts responsibly from the outset. This includes paying bills on time, keeping credit card balances low, and living within your means. If you foresee difficulty in making payments, reach out to your creditors before they turn the account over to a collection agency. Most creditors are willing to work with you to create a payment plan that prevents the account from going into collections. To further protect yourself from the negative consequences of unpaid debt, it's crucial to avoid judgments and liens. This can be achieved by maintaining open lines of communication with your creditors, settling debts before they reach the point of legal action, and seeking legal advice if you're served with a lawsuit. A judgment remains on your credit report for seven years and can severely impact your credit score, making it more difficult to obtain credit in the future.

Understanding the difference between good and bad debt, and knowing how to manage and communicate about your debts, are key components of financial health. By borrowing wisely, staying informed, and addressing debt issues promptly, you can avoid the pitfalls of bad debt and work toward achieving true financial freedom. If you find yourself struggling with debt, there are strategies you can use to regain control. One method involves paying off your smallest debts first to build momentum. Another focuses on paying off high-interest debt first to minimize the total interest paid. Whichever method you choose, the key is to have a plan and stick to it.

Understanding the terms of any credit agreements you enter into is crucial for maintaining financial health and avoiding unnecessary costs. When you take on credit, whether it's through a loan, credit card, or line of credit, you need to be fully aware of the details outlined in the agreement. This includes knowing the interest rate, repayment terms, fees, and any other conditions that may affect your financial situation. The interest rate is a fundamental aspect of any credit agreement. It determines how much you will pay in addition to the principal amount borrowed. Interest rates can be fixed or variable, with fixed rates remaining the same throughout the life of the loan and variable rates fluctuating based on market conditions. Understanding whether your rate is fixed or variable is important because it affects how much you will ultimately pay over time. For example, a credit card with a 20% annual percentage rate (APR) can result in significant interest charges if you carry a balance from month to month. As financial author Suze Orman points out, "Credit cards are not a way to extend your income; they are a way to buy things you cannot afford." Repayment terms are another critical component. These terms dictate how long you have to repay the borrowed amount and the frequency of payments. For instance, a car loan might have a term of five years with monthly payments, while a personal loan could have a term of three years with bi-weekly payments. It's essential to understand these terms to manage your budget effectively and avoid late fees or penalties. The repayment schedule should fit comfortably within your financial plan to prevent missed payments and potential damage to your credit score. Fees associated with credit agreements can include annual fees, late payment fees, and transaction fees. For example, many credit cards charge an annual fee simply for having the card, while others may impose fees for cash advances or foreign transactions. Understanding these fees can help you avoid unnecessary costs and choose credit products that align with your financial goals. As the consumer protection organization Consumer Reports highlights, "Hidden fees are often the most insidious because they chip away at your finances without your immediate realization."

Be particularly cautious of predatory lending practices, which can trap borrowers in a cycle of debt. Payday loans are a prime example of such practices. These short-term, high-interest loans are often marketed as a quick solution to urgent financial needs. However, payday loans typically come with exorbitant interest rates—often exceeding 400% APR—along with significant fees. For instance, if you take out a $500 payday loan and fail to repay it on time, you could end up paying hundreds of dollars in interest and fees. The Consumer Financial Protection Bureau (CFPB) warns, "Payday loans are expensive and are often used to address short-term cash flow issues. However, they frequently lead to a cycle of debt due to their high costs and short repayment periods." To avoid falling victim to predatory lending, consider alternative options for financial assistance. For instance, if you need a short-term loan, explore credit unions or community banks that offer lower interest rates and more favorable terms. Additionally, building an emergency fund can help you manage unexpected expenses without resorting to high-cost borrowing. Understanding the full terms of credit agreements is essential for making informed financial decisions and avoiding excessive debt. By carefully reviewing interest rates, repayment terms, and fees, and by steering clear of predatory lending practices, you can better manage your finances and protect your long-term financial well-being. As Proverbs 22:7 advises, "The rich rule over the poor, and the borrower is slave to the lender." Being knowledgeable and cautious with credit helps you maintain control over your financial future. Once you have a clear understanding of credit and how to manage it responsibly, it's essential to shift your focus to another critical aspect of financial stability: insurance. Just as credit helps you manage and leverage your financial resources, insurance provides a safety net to protect those resources from unexpected events and risks.

While often overlooked, insurance plays a crucial role in financial planning and empowerment. It serves as a fundamental tool for managing risk, offering protection against unforeseen events that could otherwise lead to significant financial hardship. By incorporating insurance into your financial strategy, you safeguard not only yourself but also your assets and loved ones from potential devastation. Insurance works by providing a safety net that helps cover the costs associated with various types of risks. For example, health insurance helps manage the financial burden of medical expenses, which can be substantial without coverage. According to the Kaiser Family Foundation, "Health insurance significantly reduces the financial strain of unexpected medical expenses and provides access to essential healthcare services." Without health insurance, a serious medical condition or accident could lead to overwhelming debt, disrupting your financial stability and well-being. Similarly, auto insurance protects you from the financial consequences of car accidents, including repair costs and liability for damages to others. In many places, having auto insurance is not just a wise choice but a legal requirement. As noted by the Insurance Information Institute, "Auto insurance helps protect against the financial consequences of vehicle accidents, providing coverage for damage to vehicles and liability for injuries or property damage caused to others."

Homeowner's insurance and renter's insurance are both designed to provide financial protection, but they cover different aspects of property ownership and rental arrangements. Understanding the distinctions between these two types of insurance is crucial for ensuring adequate coverage for your specific needs. Homeowner's insurance is designed for those who own their homes and provides comprehensive coverage for both the structure of the house and the personal property within it. This type of insurance typically includes coverage for damage to the home caused by events such as fire, storm, or vandalism, as well as liability protection in case someone is injured on your property. For example, if a fire damages your home, homeowner's insurance would cover the cost of repairs or rebuilding. According to the National Association of Insurance Commissioners, "Homeowners insurance protects against damage to your home and belongings, liability for accidents, and additional living expenses if you are temporarily displaced." Homeowner's insurance also often includes personal property coverage, which helps replace belongings like furniture, electronics, and clothing if they are stolen or damaged. For instance, if a burglary occurs and your television is stolen, homeowner's insurance would typically cover the cost of replacing it. Additionally, homeowner's insurance provides liability coverage for accidents that occur on your property, such as if a guest is injured and sues you for damages. This liability protection helps cover legal fees and potential settlements. On the other hand, renter's insurance is designed for individuals who rent their living space rather than owning it. Renter's insurance primarily covers the personal property within the rented space, such as clothing, electronics, and furniture. For example, if a fire damages your apartment and destroys your possessions, renter's insurance would help cover the cost of replacing those items. As the Insurance Information Institute explains, "Renter's insurance provides coverage for your personal belongings, liability protection, and additional living expenses if you are unable to live in your rented space due to covered damages." While renter's insurance does not cover the physical structure of the building (which is the landlord's responsibility), it does offer liability protection similar to homeowner's insurance. This means that if someone is injured in your rented space and decides to sue, renter's insurance can help cover legal expenses and damages. Additionally, renter's insurance often includes coverage for additional living expenses, which can help pay for temporary housing and other costs if your rental becomes uninhabitable due to a covered event. Homeowner's insurance and renter's insurance both provide important protection but serve different needs. Homeowner's insurance covers the structure of the home and personal property, along with liability protection, while renter's insurance focuses on protecting personal belongings and providing liability coverage within a rental property. As financial expert Suze Orman highlights, "Whether you own or rent, having insurance helps protect your assets and provides peace of mind against unexpected events." Understanding these differences ensures that you choose the right type of coverage to safeguard your financial well-being.

In addition to the essential coverage provided by homeowner's, renter's, and other forms of insurance, life insurance plays a pivotal role in financial planning and wealth management. Life insurance is designed to provide financial security for your loved ones in the event of your death, offering a financial cushion to cover living expenses, debts, and future needs. This ensures that your family can maintain their standard of living and avoid financial strain during a challenging time. As financial advisor Dave Ramsey emphasizes, "Life insurance is a crucial part of financial planning, providing peace of mind and financial security for your family's future."

Types of Life Insurance

1. Term Life Insurance: This is one of the simplest and most affordable types of life insurance. It provides coverage for a specified term, usually 10, 20, or 30 years. If the insured passes away during this term, the policy pays out a death benefit to the beneficiaries. However, if the term expires and the insured is still alive, the coverage ends, and no benefit is paid out. Term life insurance is often used to cover temporary financial obligations, such as a mortgage or education expenses for children. As noted by the Insurance Information Institute, "Term life insurance offers straightforward coverage at a lower cost, making it an ideal choice for those needing coverage for a specific period."

2. Whole Life Insurance: Unlike term life, whole life insurance provides coverage for the insured's entire lifetime, as long as premiums are paid. In addition to the death benefit, whole life policies build cash value over time, which can be borrowed against or used to pay premiums. This type of insurance is more expensive than term life but offers lifelong protection and a savings component. Financial advisor Suze Orman points out, "Whole life insurance combines death benefit protection with a savings element, providing both lifelong coverage and the opportunity to accumulate cash value."

3. Universal Life Insurance: Universal life insurance is a flexible policy that allows the insured to adjust their premium payments and death benefit amount. It also accumulates cash value, which earns interest based on current market rates. This flexibility makes universal life insurance suitable for those who want to tailor their coverage to their changing financial situation and goals. As Investopedia explains, "Universal life insurance offers the flexibility to adjust premiums and death benefits, making it a versatile option for long-term financial planning."

4. Variable Life Insurance: Variable life insurance combines life coverage with investment opportunities. Policyholders can allocate their premiums among various investment options, such as stocks and bonds. The cash value and death benefit can fluctuate based on the performance of these investments. While this offers the potential for higher returns, it also comes with increased risk. As noted by the Financial Industry Regulatory Authority (FINRA), "Variable life insurance allows policyholders to invest premiums in a variety of accounts, offering the potential for higher returns but also exposing them to market risk."

5. Indexed Universal Life Insurance: Indexed universal life insurance is similar to universal life insurance but ties the cash value growth to a stock market index, such as the S&P 500. This type of policy provides a potential for higher returns than traditional universal life insurance, with some protection against market losses. It combines the flexibility of universal life insurance with the growth potential of equity investments. According to Forbes, "Indexed universal life insurance offers the potential for higher cash value accumulation linked to market indices while providing a level of protection against market downturns."

Life insurance plays a significant role in wealth management by addressing several key areas:

Income Replacement: Life insurance provides a financial safety net for your dependents, replacing lost income and ensuring that they can continue to meet their living expenses without financial hardship.

Debt Coverage: It can be used to pay off outstanding debts, such as mortgages, car loans, or personal loans, preventing your family from having to manage these obligations alone.

Estate Planning: Life insurance can be an effective tool in estate planning, helping to cover estate taxes and ensuring that your assets are distributed according to your wishes.

Wealth Transfer: It can facilitate the transfer of wealth to heirs or beneficiaries, providing a financial legacy that supports their future needs and goals.

By integrating life insurance into your overall financial strategy, you ensure that your family's financial future is secure, even in your absence. This aligns with the biblical principle in Proverbs 13:22: "A good person leaves an inheritance for their children's children," highlighting the importance of planning ahead to provide for future generations.

Insurance also helps manage risk by enabling you to transfer the financial burden of potential losses to an insurance company. This transfer of risk allows you to focus on your financial goals without the constant worry of unforeseen expenses derailing your plans. As stated by the American Council of Life Insurers, "Insurance allows individuals and businesses to transfer the financial risk of unexpected events, thereby protecting their financial stability and enabling them to pursue their goals with confidence."

Integrating insurance into your financial planning is essential for managing risk and protecting yourself and your assets. By ensuring you have appropriate coverage for health, auto, home, and life, you create a solid foundation that shields you from potential financial shocks. As Proverbs 27:12 advises, "The prudent see danger and take refuge, but the simple keep going and pay the penalty." Embracing insurance as part of your financial strategy helps you navigate uncertainties with greater security and resilience.

There are many types of insurance to consider as part of your financial plan:

1. Health Insurance: This protects you from the potentially enormous costs of medical care. It's essential to understand your policy, including deductibles, co-pays, and coverage limits.

2. Life Insurance: This provides financial protection for your loved ones in the event of your death. There are two main types: term life insurance, which provides coverage for a specific period, and whole life insurance, which provides lifelong coverage and has an investment component.

3. Property Insurance: This includes homeowners or renters insurance, which protects your home and possessions from damage or theft.

4. Auto Insurance: This is not only legally required in most places but also protects you from the financial consequences of accidents.

5. Disability Insurance: This provides income if you're unable to work due to illness or injury. This type of insurance can be crucial in maintaining financial stability if you're unable to earn an income for an extended period.

6. Long-Term Care Insurance: This covers the cost of extended care in a nursing home or assisted living facility, or at-home care.

When considering insurance, it's important to balance the cost of premiums with the potential financial impact of being uninsured. While it may be tempting to skimp on insurance to save money in the short term, being underinsured can lead to financial ruin in the event of a major incident. As you navigate the complexities of protecting your financial well-being, it is essential to not only select the right types of insurance but also to regularly review and update your policies.

Regularly reviewing your insurance coverage is a critical aspect of maintaining financial security and ensuring that your policies align with your evolving needs. As life events such as marriage, the birth of a child, or purchasing a home occur, it's essential to reassess your insurance to make necessary adjustments. This review helps ensure that you have adequate protection and are not underinsured or overinsured, which can affect your financial stability and peace of mind. When reviewing your insurance coverage, start by examining each policy to determine if it still meets your current needs. For example, if you have recently purchased a new home, you'll need to ensure that your homeowner's insurance adequately covers the increased value of your property and any new assets you've acquired. Similarly, if your family has grown, you may need to update your life insurance to provide for additional dependents and cover any new financial responsibilities.

Here are some key aspects to consider during your insurance review:

1. Coverage Limits: Check if your coverage limits are sufficient to protect your current assets and liabilities. For instance, if you've upgraded to a larger home or acquired valuable personal property, you may need to increase your coverage limits. As insurance expert Michael Barry suggests, "Regularly reviewing your coverage limits ensures that your policy keeps pace with your evolving financial situation and protects your assets adequately."

2. Deductibles and Premiums: Evaluate whether your deductibles and premiums are still appropriate for your budget and risk tolerance. If your financial situation has changed, such as a change in income or expenses, you might need to adjust these amounts to balance affordability with coverage adequacy.

3. Beneficiary Designations: Ensure that the beneficiaries listed on your life insurance and other relevant policies are up-to-date. Major life events like marriage or divorce may necessitate changes in beneficiary designations to reflect your current wishes. According to financial planner James Lange, "Regularly updating beneficiary designations ensures that your policy benefits are distributed according to your current intentions and family situation."

4. Policy Exclusions and Limitations: Review any exclusions or limitations in your policies to understand what is not

covered. For example, some homeowner's insurance policies may exclude certain types of damage, such as flooding. Understanding these limitations can help you decide if additional coverage, such as flood insurance, is necessary.

5. Changes in Personal Circumstances: Consider how recent life changes impact your insurance needs. If you've had a child, you might need additional life insurance coverage to ensure your child's future financial needs are met. If you've recently started a home-based business, you may need to add business insurance to cover potential liabilities.

When conducting your insurance review, ask the following questions to ensure your coverage is adequate:

Does my current coverage reflect my current needs and financial situation? This question helps assess if your coverage limits, deductibles, and premiums are still appropriate based on your current assets, liabilities, and income.

Have there been any significant life changes that might impact my insurance needs? This includes recent events like marriage, the birth of a child, or purchasing a new home.

Are there any gaps or exclusions in my policy that I should be aware of? Understanding policy exclusions can help you determine if you need additional coverage or riders.

Are my beneficiary designations up-to-date and reflective of my current wishes? Regularly updating beneficiaries ensures that the benefits of your policies are distributed according to your current intentions.

Is my current insurer offering competitive rates and coverage options compared to other providers? Comparing your current policy with offerings from other insurers can help ensure you're getting the best value for your coverage.

By thoroughly reviewing your insurance coverage and asking these critical questions, you can make informed decisions to protect your financial well-being and adapt to life's changes. This proactive approach aligns with the principle of stewardship found in Proverbs 27:23: "Be diligent to know the state of your flocks and give attention to your herds," emphasizing the importance of careful management and regular assessment in maintaining financial security.

Financial literacy is not a destination, but a journey. The financial world is constantly evolving, with new products, regulations, and economic conditions emerging all the time. To stay financially empowered, it's important to commit to continuous learning. There are many resources available for improving your financial literacy. Books, podcasts, online courses, and financial blogs can all be valuable sources of information. Financial advisors can provide personalized guidance based on your specific situation. Many banks and credit unions offer free financial education programs for their customers. It's also important to stay informed about broader economic trends and how they might affect your financial situation. Understanding concepts like inflation, interest rates, and economic cycles can help you make more informed decisions about your money. Remember, financial literacy is not just about accumulating knowledge; it's about applying that knowledge to improve your financial situation. As you learn new concepts, try to implement them in your own financial life. This practical application will reinforce your learning and lead to real financial empowerment.

As you become more financially literate and empowered, consider sharing your knowledge with others. Financial literacy is a critical life skill that is often overlooked in traditional education systems. By teaching others about personal finance, you can help them avoid common pitfalls and set themselves up for financial success. This is particularly important when it comes to children and young adults. Teaching kids about money from an early age can set them up for a lifetime of financial success. This can start with simple concepts like saving a portion of their allowance, and progress to more complex topics like understanding credit and insurance as they get older.

In the workplace, employers can play a role in promoting financial literacy among their employees. This might include offering financial education programs, providing access to financial advisors, or offering benefits like retirement savings plans with employer matching. Community organizations and non-profits also play a crucial role in promoting financial literacy, particularly among underserved populations. By volunteering with or supporting these organizations, you can help promote financial empowerment in your community. Financial literacy and empowerment are essential skills in today's complex economic landscape. They provide the knowledge and confidence to make informed decisions about money, leading to greater financial security and freedom. From understanding basic concepts like budgeting and saving, to more complex topics like credit management and insurance, financial literacy covers a wide range of important skills. Building a strong financial foundation, understanding and managing credit and debt wisely, choosing appropriate insurance coverage, and committing to continuous learning are all crucial components of financial empowerment. By mastering these areas, you can take control of your financial life and work towards achieving your goals. Remember, financial literacy is not just about personal gain. By sharing your knowledge with others, you can help promote financial empowerment in your family, workplace, and community. This ripple effect can lead to broader economic stability and prosperity. The path to financial freedom may not always be easy, but with dedication, discipline, and the right knowledge, it is achievable. As you continue on this journey, stay curious, stay informed, and most importantly, stay committed to your financial goals. Your future self will thank you for the effort you put in today.

Chapter 7 Financial Literacy and Empowerment

Reflective Questions

1. What are my short-term and long-term financial goals, and how well am I currently positioned to achieve them?

2. How effectively am I tracking my income and expenses, and what changes could I make to improve my budgeting habits?

3. Am I adequately prepared for financial emergencies with a sufficient emergency savings fund, and how can I strengthen this safety net?

4. How well do I understand the terms and conditions of my credit agreements, and what steps can I take to avoid high-interest debt?

5. What is my current credit score, and what actions can I take to improve or maintain a strong credit profile?

6. Am I making informed decisions about my investments, and how can I better align my investment strategy with my risk tolerance and financial goals?

7. How often do I review and adjust my insurance coverage to ensure it meets my evolving needs, and what areas might require more attention?

8. In what ways am I actively building wealth, and how can I enhance my approach to ensure long-term financial security?

9. How do I educate myself about financial matters, and what resources or tools can I use to deepen my financial knowledge and skills?

10. How do I define financial empowerment, and what specific steps can I take to feel more in control of my financial future?

Chapter 8:
Embracing True Prosperity

True prosperity is more than the accumulation of wealth; it is a holistic state of well-being that encompasses financial stability, personal fulfillment, and a deep sense of purpose. In today's fast-paced world, many equate prosperity solely with monetary success, but true prosperity is about achieving a balanced life where financial health is just one aspect. To truly embrace prosperity, one must recognize that wealth without well-being is hollow. As the philosopher Jim Rohn once said, "Happiness is not something you postpone for the future; it is something you design for the present." This perspective challenges us to rethink our approach to wealth, encouraging us to focus on the broader spectrum of life's riches, including relationships, health, and personal growth. Consider the story of John D. Rockefeller, one of the wealthiest individuals in history. Despite his immense wealth, Rockefeller faced severe health issues in his 50s due to stress and the relentless pursuit of more wealth. It wasn't until he began to focus on giving back, philanthropy, and living a more balanced life that he found true peace and happiness. His transformation is a testament to the idea that prosperity is not just about what you have but also about how you live. Rockefeller's shift from hoarding wealth to sharing it underscores the importance of aligning financial success with a greater purpose, a key principle in embracing true prosperity. At the core of true prosperity is financial security, but this security must be built on a foundation of sound principles and values. Achieving financial independence requires more than just smart investments and savings; it demands a mindset of resilience, discipline, and a willingness to delay gratification. For example, those who practice regular saving and investing, even in small amounts, often find themselves in a stronger financial position over time compared to those who seek quick gains through high-risk ventures. This long-term approach is echoed in the words of Warren Buffett, who advised, "Do not save what is left after spending, but spend what is left after saving." This wisdom highlights the importance of prioritizing savings and investments as a pathway to financial security and, ultimately, true prosperity.

However, financial prosperity alone does not guarantee fulfillment. True prosperity involves cultivating a mindset that values experiences, relationships, and personal development just as much as financial success. This is where the concept of "wealth in all areas of life" comes into play. For example, someone who prioritizes family time, community involvement, and personal hobbies may experience a richer life than someone who focuses solely on increasing their net worth. Research has shown that people who invest time in building strong relationships and engaging in meaningful activities often report higher levels of life satisfaction, regardless of their financial status. As Albert Einstein aptly noted, "Not everything that can be counted counts, and not everything that counts can be counted." This quote reminds us that the true measures of prosperity are often intangible, found in the quality of our relationships, the joy in our daily lives, and the sense of purpose we feel. Another essential aspect of true prosperity is the ability to give back. Prosperity should not be hoarded; it should be shared. The act of giving, whether through charitable donations, volunteering, or simply offering support to others, enriches our lives and strengthens our communities. Oprah Winfrey, a self-made billionaire and philanthropist, once said, "To move forward, you have to give back." Her life is a powerful example of how prosperity, when shared, can create a ripple effect that touches countless lives. By embracing a spirit of generosity, we not only enhance the lives of others but also deepen our own sense of fulfillment and purpose. Giving back transforms prosperity from a personal achievement into a collective force for good, reinforcing the idea that true prosperity is interconnected and communal. In addition to financial security and giving back, true prosperity is deeply connected to living with intention and mindfulness. In our modern world, where distractions abound and the pressure to achieve is constant, it is easy to lose sight of what truly matters. Embracing true prosperity means making conscious choices that align with our values and long-term goals. It involves being present in the moment and appreciating the simple pleasures in life, whether it's enjoying a quiet cup of coffee in the morning or taking a walk in nature. This mindfulness can lead to a greater appreciation of what we have, reducing the constant craving for more that often drives materialistic pursuits. As mindfulness teacher Jon Kabat-Zinn explains, "The little things? The little moments? They aren't little." By paying attention to these "little moments," we can cultivate a deeper sense of contentment and joy, which are essential components of true prosperity.

Furthermore, embracing true prosperity requires a commitment to continuous learning and personal growth. Prosperity is not a static state but a dynamic process that evolves over time. Those who are truly prosperous understand the importance of expanding their knowledge, skills, and perspectives. This could mean pursuing further education, developing new talents, or seeking out new experiences that challenge and inspire us. The world-renowned author and motivational speaker Tony Robbins often speaks about the concept of "constant and never-ending improvement," which he abbreviates as CANI. This philosophy encourages us to strive for growth in all areas of our lives, recognizing that each step forward contributes to our overall prosperity. By adopting a growth mindset, we can ensure that our prosperity is not just about what we have achieved but also about who we are becoming.

True prosperity is a multifaceted concept that extends beyond financial wealth. It is about living a balanced, purposeful life where financial security, personal fulfillment, strong relationships, and a commitment to giving back all play a crucial role. To embrace true prosperity, we must cultivate a mindset that values not just the accumulation of wealth but also the joy, peace, and satisfaction that come from living in alignment with our values and purpose. As we strive for financial independence and success, let us also remember to nurture our well-being, invest in our relationships, and contribute to the greater good. In doing so, we can achieve a state of true prosperity that enriches not only our lives but also the lives of those around us.

Chapter 8. Embracing True Prosperity

Reflective Questions

1. What does wealth mean to me beyond just financial assets, and how do I define true prosperity?

2. How well am I balancing my current spending with long-term wealth-building goals?

3. What strategies am I using to diversify my investments, and how do they align with my risk tolerance and financial goals?

4. How often do I review and adjust my investment portfolio to ensure it aligns with my evolving financial objectives?

5. What role does debt play in my financial life, and how am I managing it to support my wealth-building goals?

6. How do I evaluate the difference between good debt and bad debt in my financial decisions?

7. What steps am I taking to protect my wealth from risks such as market fluctuations, inflation, or unforeseen expenses?

8. How prepared am I for financial emergencies, and what measures have I implemented to safeguard my financial stability?

9. What role does life insurance and estate planning play in my overall wealth management strategy?

10. How am I planning for retirement, and what actions can I take to ensure I can maintain my desired lifestyle in retirement?

11. How do I approach tax planning as part of my wealth management strategy to optimize my financial outcomes?

12. How effectively am I managing my real estate assets, and how do they contribute to my overall wealth-building plan?

13. What are my strategies for preserving wealth across generations, and how do I plan to pass on financial knowledge and assets to my heirs?

14. How do I stay informed about changes in the financial landscape, and what resources do I use to continue learning about wealth management?

15. How do I ensure that my financial decisions are in alignment with my personal values and long-term vision for prosperity?

16. How do I integrate gratitude and contentment into my financial journey to foster a mindset of true prosperity?

17. What impact do my financial choices have on my overall well-being, and how do they reflect my values and priorities?

18. How am I contributing to the well-being of others through my financial success, and what role does generosity play in my life?

19. What does it mean to live a life of abundance, and how do I differentiate between material wealth and true prosperity?

20. How do I measure success in my financial life, and how does that definition evolve as I grow in understanding of true prosperity?

Conclusion

As we conclude this journey through "The Prosperity Mindset: Transforming Financial Myths into Wealth Realities," it's essential to recognize that the path to true financial prosperity begins and ends within the mind. We've explored the myths that often hold us back, debunked long-standing misconceptions, and uncovered the truths that empower us to live abundantly. But knowledge alone is not enough; it's the consistent application of these principles that will lead to lasting wealth and fulfillment.

Your mindset shapes your reality. It influences your decisions, actions, and ultimately, your financial destiny. By embracing a prosperity mindset, you are choosing to see opportunities where others see obstacles, to take calculated risks where others retreat, and to build wealth not just for yourself, but for future generations. This shift in perspective is the cornerstone of transforming your financial life.

It's now time to put what you've learned into action. The strategies and insights shared in this book are tools, powerful tools, that you can use to build the life of prosperity you desire. Whether it's reevaluating your spending habits, investing in your future, or seeking out new opportunities, remember that small, consistent steps can lead to significant changes over time. The journey toward financial freedom is ongoing. There will be challenges along the way, but with a prosperity mindset, you are equipped to navigate them with confidence and resilience. Surround yourself with like-minded individuals, continue to educate yourself, and never lose sight of your goals. Remember, wealth is not just about money; it's about living a life of purpose, balance, and fulfillment. As you move forward, I encourage you to keep revisiting the principles in this book. Let them guide you as you grow and evolve. And always remember: prosperity is your birthright. It's not reserved for the few but available to all who dare to believe in their potential and take intentional action.

You've been taught how to fish, in which direction will you choose to cast your net? Will you take the knowledge and transform it into action? Will you embrace the mindset that leads to true wealth? Your financial future is a blank canvas, and you hold the brush. Create a life of abundance, generosity, and prosperity. Here's to your continued success, growth, and a future filled with limitless possibilities. Your journey to wealth realities has just begun.

"To whom much is given, much is required" (Luke 12:48). Let these words inspire you to not only seek prosperity for yourself but also to use your wealth to uplift others.

Additional Information

Common types of investing:

1. Stock Market Investing: Buying shares of publicly traded companies with the expectation of capital appreciation and dividends.

2. Bond Investing: Purchasing bonds issued by governments or corporations to earn fixed interest income over time.

3. Mutual Funds: Pools of money collected from many investors to invest in stocks, bonds, or other assets managed by professionals.

4. Exchange-Traded Funds (ETFs): Similar to mutual funds but traded on stock exchanges like individual stocks, providing diversified exposure to a specific index, sector, or commodity.

5. Real Estate Investing: Directly owning properties to generate rental income or for capital appreciation.

6. Commodities Investing: Buying physical commodities (like gold, oil) or commodity futures contracts as an investment.

7. Options and Futures: Derivative contracts that allow investors to speculate on the price movements of underlying assets.

8. Forex (Foreign Exchange) Trading: Trading currencies with the goal of profiting from changes in exchange rates.

9. Retirement Accounts: Investing through 401(k) plans, IRAs, or similar accounts with tax advantages for retirement savings.

10. Peer-to-Peer Lending: Investing money in loans to individuals or businesses through online platforms, earning interest income.

11. Angel Investing and Venture Capital: Investing in startups or early-stage companies in exchange for equity ownership.

12. Cryptocurrency Investing: Buying and holding digital currencies like Bitcoin, Ethereum, etc., with the aim of capital appreciation.

Each type of investing comes with its own risk profile, potential returns, and considerations based on individual financial goals and risk tolerance.

Deuteronomy 8:18" serves as a powerful reminder that all blessings, including the ability to produce wealth, are gifts from God. It calls believers to remember and honor God in all aspects of life, fostering a spirit of gratitude, humility, and faithful obedience."

Riches vs. Wealth: Understanding the Difference

Riches refer to an abundance of money, assets, or material possessions and can be quantified through one's assets.

- Can be fleeting
- Fluctuate with economic conditions
- Seen as a status symbol
- May lead to materialism
- Can be acquired quickly either through inheritance, luck or sudden financial gain

Impact

- May bring temporary happiness
- Can lead to stress
- May isolate individuals if relationships or personal development is not a focus

Perspective

- Focused on external accumulation
- Can be dependent on external factors

Wealth is much broader than riches because it encompasses more than just financial assets. It includes health, relationships, knowledge, and overall well-being. Unlike riches, wealth is not always quantifiable, as it involves intangible assets and the quality of life.

- Is more stable and sustainable over time
- Involves a holistic approach to life, i.e. long-term security
- Built over time through consistent effort, wise investments and personal growth

Impact

- Promotes a balanced and fulfilling life
- Encourages the development of meaningful relationships, personal growth and a sense of purpose
- Leads to lasting contentment and a positive impact on one's community and environment

Perspective

- Focused on internal fulfillment and overall quality of life
- More resilient on external changes due to a diversified approach to life and resources

Generational Wealth

What is Generational Wealth?

Generational wealth refers to assets and financial resources that are passed down from one generation to the next, providing long-term economic stability and opportunities for descendants. It encompasses not only monetary assets but also investments, property, and sometimes values or financial knowledge that contribute to enduring family prosperity.

Here are various forms of generational wealth:

Financial Assets

1. Cash Savings: Liquid assets held in savings accounts.

2. Stocks and Bonds: Investments in the stock market and fixed-income securities.

3. Mutual Funds and ETFs: Pooled investment vehicles providing diversified exposure.

4. Retirement Accounts: 401(k)s, IRAs, and other pension funds.

5. Trust Funds: Legal entities holding and managing assets for beneficiaries.

Real Estate

1. Primary Residences: Family homes passed down through generations.

2. Vacation Properties: Secondary homes or vacation rentals.

3. Rental Properties: Residential or commercial properties generating rental income.

4. Land: Undeveloped land that may appreciate over time or be used for various purposes.

Business Interests

1. Family Businesses: Ownership and management of family-operated companies.

2. Equity in Private Companies: Stakes in private enterprises that may grow in value.

Valuable Physical Assets

1. Precious Metals: Gold, silver, and other valuable metals.

2. Jewelry: High-value pieces that can be passed down.

3. Art Collections: Paintings, sculptures, and other collectible art.

4. Antiques: Valuable and historic items.

Intellectual Property

1. Patents: Legal rights to inventions.

2. Trademark: Brand names, logos, and other identifiers.

3. Copyrights: Rights to literary, musical, and artistic works.

Education and Knowledge

1. Education Funds: Savings accounts like 529 plans dedicated to future education expenses.

2. Knowledge and Skills: Expertise and skills passed down through education and training.

Insurance Policies

1. Life Insurance: Policies that provide financial support to beneficiaries.

2. Annuities: Contracts that provide periodic payments to beneficiaries.

Social Capital and Networks

1. Professional Networks: Connections and relationships that provide opportunities and support.

2. Reputation and Name: A well-established family reputation that can open doors and create opportunities.

Estate Planning Instruments

1. Wills: Legal documents outlining the distribution of assets.

2. Trusts: Arrangements for managing and distributing assets according to specific terms.

3. Power of Attorney: Legal authority granted to manage the affairs of another person.

Other Forms

1. Heirlooms: Items of sentimental value passed down through generations.

2. Cultural and Family Traditions: Practices and values that contribute to a family's identity and cohesion.

Generational wealth encompasses a wide array of assets and resources that contribute to the long-term financial health and stability of future generations, ensuring they have the means and opportunities to thrive.

Proverbs 13:22 (NIV):

"A good person leaves an inheritance for their children's children, but a sinner's wealth is stored up for the righteous."

This verse highlights the importance of not only providing for one's immediate offspring but also considering the welfare of future generations. It emphasizes the value of long-term planning and the lasting impact of a person's life and actions.

What is Legacy?

Legacy refers to anything handed down from the past, as from an ancestor or predecessor. It encompasses both tangible and intangible elements that an individual leaves behind for future generations. This includes not only material wealth but also values, traditions, knowledge, and impacts made on others' lives.

Ways to Create a Legacy for Your Children

1. Financial Planning and Wealth Management:

- Savings and Investments: Establish savings accounts, stocks, bonds, and other investment portfolios.
- Retirement Funds: Ensure you have sufficient retirement savings to avoid burdening your children.
- Real Estate: Invest in property that can be passed down.
- Life Insurance: Purchase life insurance policies to provide financial security for your family.
- Trust Funds: Create trusts to manage and protect assets for future generations.

2. Education:

- Education Funds: Set up savings plans like 529 plans for your children's education.
- Value of Learning: Instill a love for learning and the importance of education.

3. Values and Morals:

- Teach Values: Impart important values such as honesty, integrity, and compassion.
- Lead by Example: Demonstrate ethical behavior and decision-making in your daily life.

4. Family Traditions and Culture:

- Celebrate Traditions: Maintain and celebrate family traditions and cultural practices.
- Document Family History: Preserve stories, photographs, and records of your family's history.

5. Health and Wellness:

- Healthy Lifestyle: Promote and model a healthy lifestyle, including proper nutrition and regular exercise.
- Emotional Support: Provide emotional support and create a nurturing environment.

6. Knowledge and Skills:

- Teach Practical Skills: Equip your children with practical skills such as cooking, budgeting, and problem-solving.
- Professional Guidance: Offer advice and mentorship regarding career and professional development.

7. Spiritual Foundation:

- Faith and Beliefs: Share and practice your faith or spiritual beliefs.
- Community Involvement: Encourage participation in community service and spiritual gatherings.

8. Social Capital and Networks:

- Build Connections: Introduce your children to your social and professional networks.
- Community Engagement: Foster a sense of community involvement and responsibility.

9. Philanthropy and Service:

- Volunteerism: Involve your children in volunteer work and charitable activities.
- Charitable Giving: Create a culture of giving by donating to causes you care about.

10. Legacy Projects:

- Create Lasting Works: Write a book, establish a foundation, or create other lasting contributions.
- Support Causes: Champion causes or initiatives that align with your values and passions

The main differences between legacy and generational wealth are:

1. Scope:

- Legacy wealth typically refers to passing down financial assets and property.
- Generational wealth has a broader scope, including financial assets, property, businesses, education, values, and opportunities.

2. Timeframe:

- Legacy wealth often focuses on immediate inheritance or transfer to the next generation.
- Generational wealth aims to create lasting financial stability across multiple generations.

3. Purpose:

- Legacy wealth is primarily about preserving and transferring accumulated wealth.
- Generational wealth emphasizes creating sustainable financial growth and opportunities for future generations.

4. Strategy:

- Legacy wealth may involve estate planning and tax-efficient wealth transfer.
- Generational wealth strategies often include education, entrepreneurship, investment knowledge, and financial literacy.

5. Impact:

- Legacy wealth can provide immediate financial benefits to heirs.
- Generational wealth aims to break cycles of poverty and create long-term socioeconomic advancement for families.

Deuteronomy 8:18 (NIV)

"But remember the LORD your God, for it is he who gives you the ability to produce wealth, and so confirms his covenant, which he swore to your ancestors, as it is today."

Commentary:

Deuteronomy 8:18 is part of Moses' speech to the Israelites as they prepare to enter the Promised Land. Moses reminds them of their journey through the wilderness, the lessons they have learned, and the importance of obedience to God. This verse serves as a crucial reminder of the source of their blessings and prosperity.

"But remember the LORD your God"

Moses emphasizes the importance of remembering God in all circumstances, especially in times of prosperity. This call to remembrance is a recurring theme in Deuteronomy, underscoring the need for constant gratitude and acknowledgement of God's role in their lives. Forgetting God leads to pride and a false sense of self-sufficiency, which can result in turning away from His commandments.

"For it is he who gives you the ability to produce wealth"

This phrase highlights that all abilities, including the capacity to generate wealth, come from God. It is not merely human effort or intelligence that leads to prosperity, but God's provision and empowerment. This recognition fosters humility and dependence on God, rather than pride in one's own achievements.

"And so, confirms his covenant, which he swore to your ancestors"

The ability to produce wealth is tied to God's covenant with the Israelites. By blessing them with the means to prosper, God is fulfilling His promises made to their forefathers, such as Abraham, Isaac, and Jacob. This reinforces the idea that God's faithfulness is enduring, and His covenantal promises are reliable.

"As it is today"

Moses concludes by affirming that God's faithfulness and provision are evident in the present. The current blessings the Israelites experience are a direct result of God's ongoing commitment to His covenant. This serves as a reminder that God's promises are not just historical but are actively being fulfilled in their lives.

Application:

1. Gratitude and Humility:

Believers are reminded to stay grateful and humble, acknowledging that all their abilities and successes come from God. This fosters a mindset of dependence on God rather than self-reliance.

2. Faithfulness to God:

Remembering God's role in their prosperity encourages believers to remain faithful and obedient to His commandments, recognizing that their blessings are tied to their relationship with Him.

3. Generational Faithfulness:

The verse highlights the importance of God's covenant across generations. Believers are encouraged to see their blessings as part of a broader divine plan and to honor God's faithfulness through their actions.

4. Continual Remembrance:

Goal-Setting Worksheet

1. Goal Title:

Name your goal. Be specific about what you want to achieve.

2. Goal Description:

Provide a detailed description of the goal. Explain what building generational wealth means to you and why it's important.

3. SMART Criteria:

Specific: Clearly define what you want to achieve.

Measurable: Identify how you will measure progress and success.

Achievable: Assess whether the goal is realistic given your current resources and constraints.

Relevant: Ensure the goal aligns with your long-term vision and values.

Time-bound: Set a deadline or timeframe for achieving the goal.

4. Steps to Achieve the Goal:

Outline the specific actions you need to take to reach your goal. Break these into smaller, manageable tasks.

5. Resources Needed:

List the resources, tools, or support you need to achieve your goal. This could include financial resources, educational materials, or professional advice.

6. Potential Obstacles:

Identify possible challenges or barriers you might encounter and plan how to address them.

7. Accountability Plan:

Determine how you will hold yourself accountable. This could involve regular check-ins, progress reviews, or enlisting a mentor or accountability partner.

8. Success Indicators:

Define what success looks like for this goal. Include specific metrics or outcomes that indicate you have achieved your goal.

9. Reflection and Adjustment:

Set aside time to periodically review your progress and make any necessary adjustments to your plan.

10. Affirmations and Motivations:

Include positive affirmations or motivational statements to keep you inspired and focused on your goal.

Example of a Goal Set Around Building Generational Wealth

1. Goal Title:

Establish a Family Trust Fund

2. Goal Description:

Create and fund a family trust fund to ensure financial security and provide long-term wealth for future generations. The trust will be designed to support educational expenses, business investments, and retirement funds for my children and grandchildren.

3. SMART Criteria:

Specific: I will set up a family trust fund with an initial contribution of $100,000 and create a detailed plan for its management and growth.

Measurable: I will track the growth of the trust fund through quarterly financial reports and ensure it meets its annual growth targets.

Achievable: I will work with a financial advisor and legal expert to establish the trust fund and make initial investments.

Relevant: This goal aligns with my vision of providing lasting financial security for my family and fostering a legacy of wealth.

Time-bound: The trust fund will be fully established and funded within 12 months.

4. Steps to Achieve the Goal:

1. Research and select a reputable financial advisor and attorney specializing in trust funds.

2. Develop a detailed plan for the trust fund's structure and investment strategy.

3. Make an initial contribution of $100,000 to the trust fund.

4. Review and adjust the trust fund's investments quarterly.

5. Educate family members about the trust fund and its benefits.

5. Resources Needed:

Financial advisor

Estate planning attorney

Initial funding of $100,000

Educational materials on trust fund management

6. Potential Obstacles:

High setup costs or fees

Complex legal requirements

Market volatility affecting investment growth

7. Accountability Plan:

Schedule quarterly meetings with the financial advisor to review the trust fund's performance.

Keep a progress journal and set reminders to evaluate and adjust the plan as needed.

8. Success Indicators:

The trust fund is established and operational within the 12-month timeframe.

The fund grows according to the projected annual growth rate.

Positive feedback and understanding from family members regarding the trust fund's benefits.

9. Reflection and Adjustment:

Conduct an annual review of the trust fund's performance and make adjustments based on market conditions and family needs.

10. Affirmations and Motivations:

I am creating a lasting legacy of financial security for my family.

Every step I take brings me closer to building a prosperous future for generations to come

This worksheet provides a structured approach to setting and achieving goals related to building generational wealth. By following these steps and regularly reviewing progress, individuals can create a solid foundation for long-term financial success and legacy-building.

Establishing a Budget

1. Budget Title:

Name your budget (e.g., "Monthly Household Budget," "Annual Family Budget").

2. Income Sources:

List all sources of income, including salaries, side jobs, investments, and any other sources.

Example:

Salary: $3,500

Freelance Work: $500

Investment Income: $200

3. Fixed Expenses:

Identify and list all fixed expenses that occur regularly and are typically consistent in amount.

Example :

Rent/Mortgage : $1,200

Utilities : $150

Internet : $60

Insurance: $100

4. Variable Expenses:

List expenses that can fluctuate month-to-month and vary in amount.

Example:

Groceries: $400

Transportation: $200

Dining Out: $150

Entertainment: $100

5. Savings and Investments:

Determine how much you plan to allocate towards savings and investments each month.

Example:

Emergency Fund: $200

Retirement Savings: $300

Investment Account: $150

6. Debt Repayment:

Include any debt payments you need to make, such as credit card payments or loans.

Example:

Credit Card Payment: $150

Student Loan: $200

7. Total Monthly Income:

Calculate the total of all income sources.

8. Total Monthly Expenses:

Add up all fixed, variable, savings, and debt repayment expenses.

9. Balance Calculation:

Subtract total monthly expenses from total monthly income to determine your monthly balance.

Formula: Total Monthly Income - Total Monthly Expenses = Monthly Balance

Example: $4,200 (Income) - $2,560 (Expenses) = $1,640 (Balance)

10. Budget Review and Adjustments:

Periodically review your budget to ensure it aligns with your financial goals and make adjustments as necessary.

Schedule: Weekly/Monthly

11. Financial Goals:

Outline short-term and long-term financial goals you want to achieve through budgeting.

Example:

Short-Term Goal: Save $1,000 for a vacation in 6 months.

Long-Term Goal: Save $20,000 for a down payment on a house in 3 years.

12. Accountability and Tracking:

Plan how you will track your spending and stay accountable to your budget.

Methods: Budgeting app, spreadsheet, monthly review

13. Reflection and Notes:

Reflect on any challenges you faced while setting up the budget and note any insights or adjustments needed.

Example: Noticed higher grocery expenses, plan to adjust budget or find ways to reduce costs.

"A budget is telling your money where to go instead of wondering where it went." John C. Maxwell

Example Completed Budget:

1. Budget Title:

Monthly Household Budget

2. Income Sources:

Salary: $3,500

Freelance Work: $500

Investment Income: $200

3. Fixed Expenses:

Rent : $1,200

Utilities : $150

Internet : $60

Insurance : $100

4. Variable Expenses :

Groceries: $400

Transportation: $200

Dining Out: $150

Entertainment: $100

5. Savings and Investments:

Emergency Fund: $200

Retirement Savings: $300

Investment Account: $150

6. Debt Repayment:

Credit Card Payment: $150

Student Loan: $200

7. Total Monthly Income:

$4,200

8. Total Monthly Expenses:

Fixed Expenses: $1,510

Variable Expenses: $850

Savings and Investments: $650

Debt Repayment: $350

Total Expenses: $3,360

9. Balance Calculation:

$4,200 (Income) - $3,360 (Expenses) = $840 (Balance)

10. Budget Review and Adjustments:

Review budget monthly, adjust as necessary.

11. Financial Goals:

Short-Term Goal: Save $1,000 for vacation in 6 months.

Long-Term Goal: Save $20,000 for a house down payment in 3 years.

12. Accountability and Tracking:

Use budgeting app for tracking, review monthly.

13. Reflection and Notes:

Higher grocery expenses noted; adjust budget or reduce costs.

This worksheet will help you set up and maintain a budget that supports your financial goals and provides a clear picture of your income and expenses.

Mindset Matters Affirmations

1. I am deserving of unlimited wealth and abundance.

2. Money flows to me easily and effortlessly.

3. I am open to receiving all the wealth life offers me.

4. I attract prosperity and success in all areas of my life.

5. My wealth is constantly increasing as I align with abundance.

6. I am a magnet for financial opportunities.

7. I release all limiting beliefs about money and embrace a prosperous mindset.

8. I am in control of my financial destiny.

9. Every day, I am becoming richer, happier, and more fulfilled.

10. I use my wealth to create positive change in the world.

11. I am worthy of financial security and peace of mind.

12. I believe in my ability to create wealth and abundance.

13. I am grateful for the abundance that I have and the abundance on its way.

14. I am financially free and live a life of purpose and passion.

15. I am smart with my money and make wise financial decisions.

16. Wealth constantly flows into my life from multiple sources.

17. I trust in my ability to create and sustain wealth.

18. I am aligned with the energy of wealth and abundance.

19. My positive mindset attracts financial success.

20. I am open to new avenues of income and abundance.

21. I am the architect of my financial future.

The Prosperity Mindset

22. I choose to focus on abundance and prosperity.

23. I am confident in my ability to generate wealth.

24. I am grateful for the wealth that is continuously flowing into my life.

25. I am financially empowered, independent, and secure.

26. I attract wealth by being my authentic self.

27. I am a prosperous person who is always attracting success and wealth.

28. I am worthy of abundance and prosperity.

29. I attract wealth-building opportunities every day.

30. My financial decisions are wise and informed.

31. Wealth is a natural state for me.

32. I release all limiting beliefs about money.

33. My relationship with money is healthy and positive.

34. My wealth mindset attracts successful people into my life.

35. I am skilled at managing and growing my wealth.

36. I am skilled at managing and growing my wealth.

37. My actions align with my wealth goals.

38. My prosperity mindset opens doors to new levels of success.

39. I am creating a legacy of wealth and abundance.

Use these affirmations regularly to reinforce a mindset of abundance and to support your journey toward wealth transformation.

About the Writer

As a Realtor (DRE 02127722) with a deep commitment to ethics and integrity, I bring a wealth of experience and passion to the real estate industry. My journey in helping others achieve their dreams extends beyond real estate, as I also founded Gyfted Inc. in 2010, a nonprofit organization dedicated to making a positive impact on the lives of others. Guided by my personal Mission Statement to impact the lives of others through the greater good, I strive to infuse this purpose into all my endeavors.

In addition to my work in real estate and philanthropy, I established Cooks' Enterprise for Growth Promotion, LLC, a consulting and training business aimed at empowering individuals to reach their full potential. My diverse interests include reading, gardening, photography, traveling, and most importantly, spending quality time with my children, family, and friends. These hobbies not only bring joy and balance to my life but also inspire me to continue growing personally and professionally, all while staying true to my mission of serving others.

Notes

14 Most Common Myths About Becoming Wealthy | FinanceBuzz

The 8 Biggest Myths About Wealth, Poverty, and Free Enterprise | Discovery Institute

There Are Only 7 Black Billionaires in the United States - Business Insider

9 Black Millionaires Who Built Wealth Outside Of Sports And Entertainment - AfroTech

pnas201011492 1..5 (princeton.edu)

Money only buys happiness for a certain amount - Purdue University News

Education pays, 2022 : Career Outlook: U.S. Bureau of Labor Statistics (bls.gov)

Investment Strategy: Ways to Invest and Factors to Consider (investopedia.com)

Recommended Reading

The Bible (NKJV)

"The Intelligent Investor" by Benjamin Graham and David Dodd (1949)

"The Millionaire Next Door" by Thomas J. Stanley and William D. Danko (1996)

"The Richest Man in Babylon" by George S. Clason (1926)

"Think and Grow Rich" by Napoleon Hill (1937)

"Atomic Habits: An Easy & Proven Way to Build Good Habits & Break Bad Ones" by James Clear (2018)

"The Psychology of Money: Timeless Lessons on Wealth, Greed, and Happiness" by Morgan Housel (2020)

"The Compound Effect" by Darren Hardy(2010,2020)